THE 16-BAR THEATRE AUDITION

100 SONGS EXCERPTED FOR SUCCESSFUL AUDITIONS

COMPILED AND EDITED BY MICHAEL DANSICKER

ISBN 0-634-06343-X

HAL•LEONARD® CORPORATION

7777 W. BLUEMOUND RD. P.O. BOX 13819 MILWAUKEE, WI 53213

Visit Hal Leonard Online at
www.halleonard.com

CONTENTS

SHOW INDEX

PREFACE

After completing coursework in musical theatre degree programs at universities and conservatories, a very large number of musical theatre graduates, along with other young hopefuls, head for New York City. Their ultimate goal, of course, is a career in the professional musical theatre. Most young actors do not get immediate representation from agents or managers, who can secure for their clients a private appointment with a show's creative team. The standard "open singer's call" has become the most readily available opportunity for thousands of aspiring performers. It provides actors a chance to be heard and considered for work in various venues, from theme park/cruise line shows to Equity Broadway productions.

While directors, choreographers and casting offices are always anxious to discover new talent, audition time continues to be severely limited. Massive turnouts have become "the norm." In order to accommodate the crowds, the audition monitor will frequently announce the casting director's request for a 16-bar excerpt at a singing call. The concept of editing music for auditions becomes a frightening prospect to those not experienced in streamlining their selection on short notice. It is a task that takes musical experience and some careful thought!

WHY 16 BARS?

In the world of popular song writing, the standard 32-bar song form (AABA) has been the backbone of composition for decades. In this context, a 16-bar excerpt would imply half of a song. Prior to about 1970, Broadway shows were vehicles to supply the world with dance tunes and popular music. While the musical selections served the plot and characters of their shows, the songs were also written to have an extended life outside of the theatre. Today there is virtually no crossover from Broadway to the popular music market. Contemporary theatre composers and lyricists do not adhere to traditional structures, commercial form, or content in their work. Their writing faithfully serves the drama they are musicalizing, but it is not easily consolidated for an audition excerpt.

It is not always easy to decide on a 16-bar selection from a song. *The choice should not be arbitrary. You should always choose the best 16 bars!* This could be the verse, the bridge of the song, or an extended coda tagged on to your selected piece. You have to find out what works best for you. Your selection should time between 20 and 30 seconds. *No longer!* In most cases 16 bars is the right amount of music, although occasionally 32 bars will be more appropriate if the selection is in a very fast cut time, or "in 1." If you can communicate effectively to the audition panel in a shorter cutting, such as 8 or 12 bars, then do so! The piano introduction to your singing should be very limited, usually a one-note "bell tone" or one bar. It is not out of line to request your starting pitch when you speak with the pianist. Make sure you clearly communicate the tempo to the audition pianist. Your music should be clearly marked. Any transposition should be neatly written out. Do not expect the accompanist to transpose at sight. Material from showcases, camp shows and college revues should be left at home. Discordant arrangements and bizarre novelty tunes are of little use in 16-bar auditions. Of course, pass over songs that include extended orchestral solos.

BASIC PRESENTATION

You must impart your complete understanding of the music and lyrics you have selected. Your negotiation of the musical phrase and ability to be specific with acting elements are very important. Good singing technique is, of course, essential (placement, breath control and pitch). Your connection with the dramatic integrity of the piece is also important. The song should be presented honestly and thoughtfully. Be familiar with the shows you are auditioning for! Your music should reflect the style and spirit of the musical being cast. Dialects should be avoided; unless told otherwise, sing in English! It is never wise to interpolate unlikely notes to show off the upper limits of your vocal range. If a composer, or a firm performing tradition, has given an optional high note, feel free to use it. However, a disembodied "howl" with no cohesive relation to the phrase will surely not work favorably for you. While the rigor of a competitive audition experience can take its toll, always impart a sense of total commitment to your work, and the joy of being a musical theatre actor.

VOCAL RANGES

On Broadway today, the baritone has become a bari-tenor. A solid high F is imperative; a G is better. Basses should have an audible low F. Sopranos are sometimes asked for high D's, and belters now go as high as F. Tenors many times are asked for high C. But these are the extreme limits of range. At best, a 16-bar selection serves as an introduction to your vocal/acting skills. Do what is comfortable for you. If you are to be considered for a position in a production, further exploration of your vocal ability will take place in a callback situation. *You can't show everything in 16 bars!* Tenors should feel free to use selections from the baritone volume. Ladies should be ready to show the legit (soprano) and belt aspects of their voices if asked. Always have an alternate selection ready.

DANCERS

The dancer's call is a bit different than an open singer's call. The singing portion of the dancer audition is held only after the dancers have learned the presented movement combination and made their way through an elimination process. While many dancers in New York can hold their own at any singer call, the creative team will be a bit more flexible with dancers for the singing portion of the audition.

THE SELECTIONS IN THESE VOLUMES

The repertoire of the Broadway musical remains abundant and diversified, but large segments of material remain under-utilized. I have included selections from Broadway musicals, operettas, and pop hits. I gravitated to writers of outstanding talent and exceptional merit. A well-written song is a tremendous asset to any performer. No individual will be able to use all 100 excerpts in a particular anthology! There are songs that demand leading lady and leading man stature, as well as character and comic selections. There are pieces that have enormous vocal range, and many that are just rhythmic and charming. It is your job to peruse the contents and find what you consider the right songs for your needs. I have heard all of this material used to great advantage at many auditions. I have attempted to edit and indicate the most effective cuttings, trying to avoid phrase interruption. I have chosen what I feel are the most suitable keys, however, do not be afraid to experiment with the key (but have it written out to take to the audition!). Do not be afraid to use a song that is commonly heard at auditions. It is important that your "take" on the material be intelligent and professional. Every actor is unique, and those listening to your audition will not object to hearing a song again.

AUDITIONING

The only way to secure a job in legitimate musical theatre is through a live audition. Everyone auditions! Some actors audition better than others. The audition process is one that takes time to hone, polish and perfect. While many successful film and television actors secure continuous employment via a compilation reel of their media exposure, stage actors must book via a live audition. Be honest in evaluating the success of each audition, and study how it can be improved in the future. Also take note of the people you are auditioning for, and keep this information in a journal for future reference. Continue studying voice and working with a vocal coach. Dance and acting classes are essential for keeping your work sharp and at a high, professional level.

I hope these editions of 16-bar selections will be helpful to actors planning to audition for any musical show. *It is very important that you also learn the entire song after you master the 16-bar excerpt.* There is always a chance that someone on the creative team will say, "That was great; let's hear the whole song!" *Be prepared.*

Michael Dansicker
New York City
December, 2003

MICHAEL DANSICKER has worked as arranger, composer, musical director, and pianist on over 100 Broadway and Off-Broadway productions, from *Grease* (1975) to *Dance of the Vampires* (2003). He has composed original music for over a dozen plays in New York, including *The Glass Menagerie* (revival with Jessica Tandy) and *Total Abandon* (with Richard Dreyfus), and musically supervised the Royal Shakespeare Company transfers of *Piaf*, *Good*, and *Les Liaisons Dangereuses*. He served as vocal consultant to the hit films *Elf* (New Line Cinema), *Analyze That!* (Warner Bros.), and *Meet the Parents* (Universal), and also scored the dance sequences for Paramount's comedy classic *Brain Donors* (starring John Turturro). In the world of concert dance, he has composed and scored pieces for Twyla Tharp, American Ballet Theatre, Geoffrey Holder, Mikhail Baryshnikov, and The Joffrey, as well as serving as pianist to Jerome Robbins and Agnes DeMille. Michael currently works as creative consultant to Walt Disney Entertainment. He composed the music for "The Audition Suite" (lyrics by Martin Charnin), published by Hal Leonard Corporation. As a vocal coach, he works with the top talent in New York and Hollywood (including Sony's pop division). As an audition pianist, he works regularly with important casting directors on both coasts, and for 15 years has played all major auditions for Jay Binder, the "dean" of Broadway casting. Mr. Dansicker's original music is licensed by BMI. He holds a MA from the Catholic University of America.

AND THIS IS MY BELOVED
from *Kismet*

Words and Music by ROBERT WRIGHT
and GEORGE FORREST
(Music Based on Themes of A. Borodin)

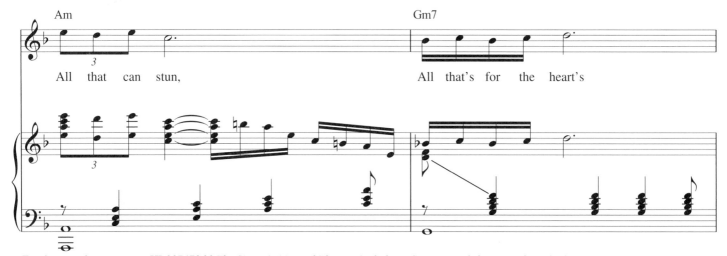

For the complete song see: HL00747066 *The Singer's Musical Theatre Anthology, Soprano Vol. 2 (Revised),* and other sources.

ART IS CALLING FOR ME
from *The Enchantress*

Music by VICTOR HERBERT
Lyrics by HARRY B. SMITH

For the complete song see: HL00747066 *The Singer's Musical Theatre Anthology, Soprano Vol. 2 (Revised),* and other sources.

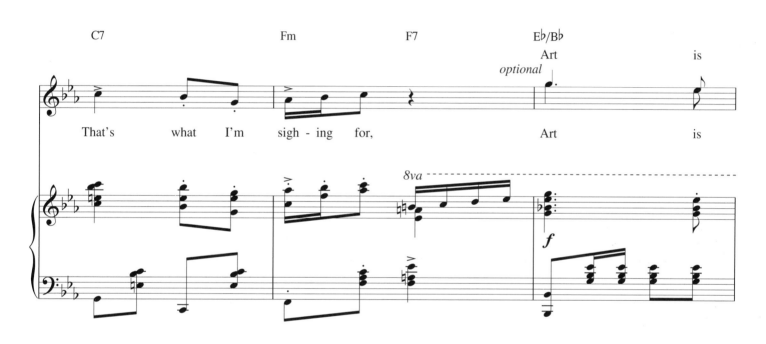

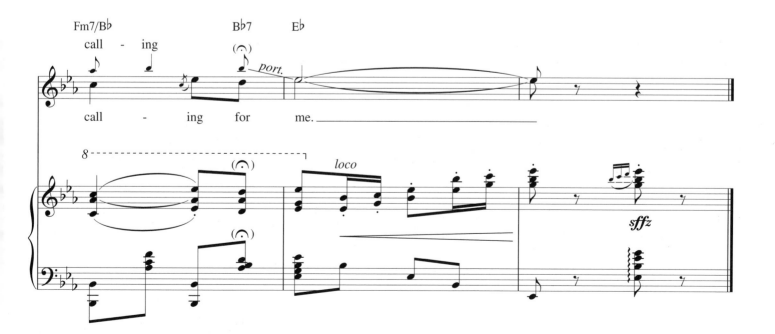

AS SIMPLE AS THAT

from *Milk and Honey*

Music and Lyric by
JERRY HERMAN

For the complete song see: HL00385217 *The Jerry Herman Songbook.*

BAUBLES, BANGLES AND BEADS

Excerpt

from *Kismet*

Words and Music by ROBERT WRIGHT
and GEROGE FORREST
(Music Based on Themes of A. Borodin)

I'll glit - ter and gleam so,

Make some - bod - y dream so That some - day he may

buy me a ring, ring - a - ling - a, I've heard that's where it leads, _____

_____ Wear - ing bau - bles, ban - gles and beads.

For the complete song see: HL00360228 *Kismet* vocal selections, and other sources.

16
Excerpt

BEFORE I GAZE AT YOU AGAIN
from *Camelot*

Words by ALAN JAY LERNER
Music by FREDERICK LOEWE

For the complete song see: HL00740122 *The Singer's Musical Theatre Anthology, Soprano Vol. 3.*

Excerpt

BILLIE
from *George M!*

Words and Music by
GEORGE M. COHAN

Moderately slow

They think it so queer that a girl should ap-pear, their il-lu-sions I fear I de-stroy. Here is the rea-son my name's Bil-lie, My par-ents ex-pect-ed a boy.

For the complete song see: HL00008203 *George M!* vocal selections.

Excerpt

CHILDREN OF THE WIND
from *Rags*

Lyric by STEPHEN SCHWARTZ
Music by CHARLES STROUSE

For the complete song see: HL00313232 *Rags* vocal selections.

CLIMB EV'RY MOUNTAIN
from *The Sound of Music*

Lyrics by OSCAR HAMMERSTEIN II
Music by RICHARD RODGERS

For the complete song see: HL00361071 *The Singer's Musical Theatre Anthology, Soprano Vol. 1 (Revised),* and other sources.

Excerpt

A COCK-EYED OPTIMIST
from *South Pacific*

Lyrics by OSCAR HAMMERSTEIN II
Music by RICHARD RODGERS

For the complete song see: HL00312400 *South Pacific* vocal selections, and other sources.

Excerpt

COME HOME

from *Allegro*

Lyrics by OSCAR HAMMERSTEIN II
Music by RICHARD RODGERS

For the complete song see: HL00361071 *The Singer's Musical Theatre Anthology, Soprano Vol. 1 (Revised),* and other sources.

Excerpt

COMES ONCE IN A LIFETIME

from *Subways Are For Sleeping*

Words by BETTY COMDEN and ADOLPH GREEN
Music by JULE STYNE

For the complete song see: HL00361198 *The Songs of Jule Styne,* and other sources.

CRY LIKE THE WIND

from *Do Re Mi*

Words by BETTY COMDEN and ADOLPH GREEN
Music by JULE STYNE

Excerpt

DANCING ON THE CEILING
from *Simple Simon*

Words by LORENZ HART
Music by RICHARD RODGERS

For the complete song see: HL00307940*Rodgers and Hart – A Musical Anthology,* and other sources.

DO I HEAR A WALTZ?

from *Do I Hear a Waltz?*

Music by RICHARD RODGERS
Lyrics by STEPHEN SONDHEIM

For the complete song see: HL00312115 *Do I Hear a Waltz?* vocal selections, and other sources.

DON'T LIKE GOODBYES
from *House of Flowers*

Lyric by TRUMAN CAPOTE and HAROLD ARLEN
Music by HAROLD ARLEN

For the complete song see: HL00383780 *House of Flowers* vocal selections, and other sources.

Excerpt

GETTING MARRIED TODAY
from *Company*

Music and Lyrics by
STEPHEN SONDHEIM

Excerpt

FALLING IN LOVE WITH LOVE

from *The Boys from Syracuse*

Words by LORENZ HART
Music by RICHARD RODGERS

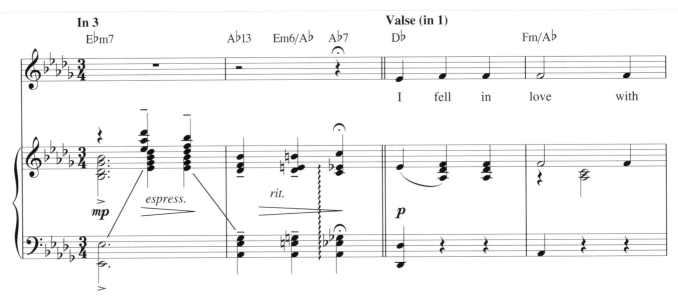

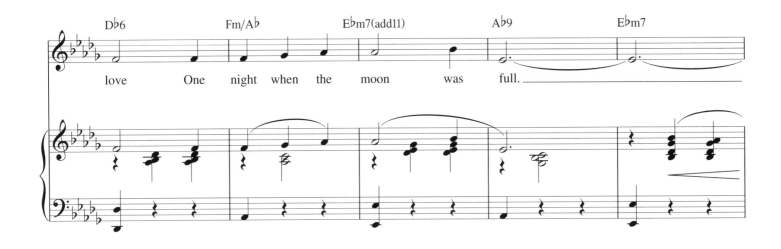

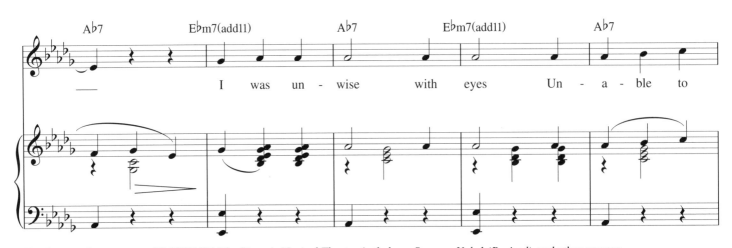

For the complete song see: HL00361071 *The Singer's Musical Theatre Anthology, Soprano Vol. 1 (Revised),* and other sources.

GLAD TO BE UNHAPPY
from *On Your Toes*

Words by LORENZ HART
Music by RICHARD RODGERS

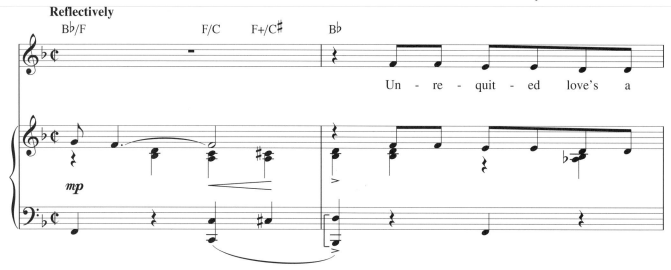

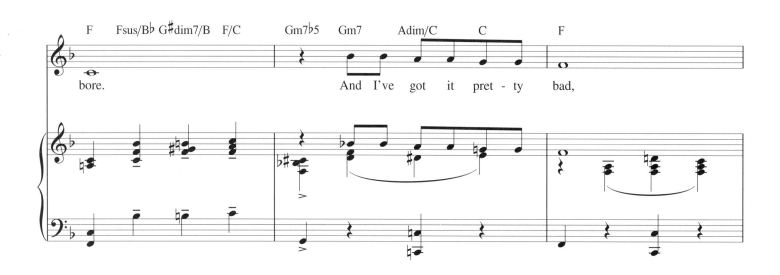

For the complete song see: HL00312299 *On Your Toes* vocal selections, and other sources.

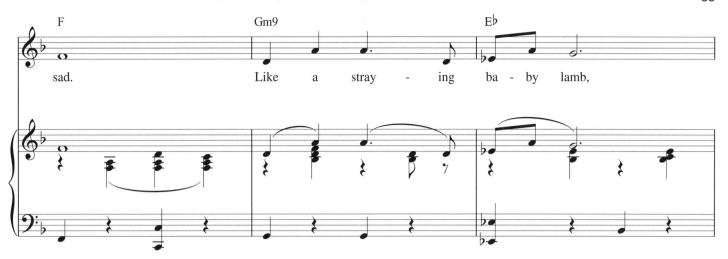

sad.　　Like a stray - ing ba - by lamb,

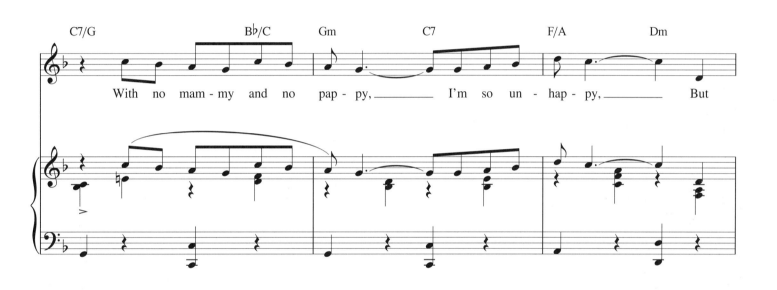

With no mam - my and no pap - py,_____ I'm so un - hap - py,_____ But

oh, so glad!_____

Excerpt

THE GOLDEN RAM
from *Two By Two*

Lyrics by MARTIN CHARNIN
Music by RICHARD RODGERS

For the complete song see: HL00361071 *The Singer's Musical Theatre Anthology, Soprano Vol. 1 (Revised).*

Excerpt

HE WAS TOO GOOD TO ME

from *Simple Simon*

Words by LORENZ HART
Music by RICHARD RODGERS

Slowly, with feeling

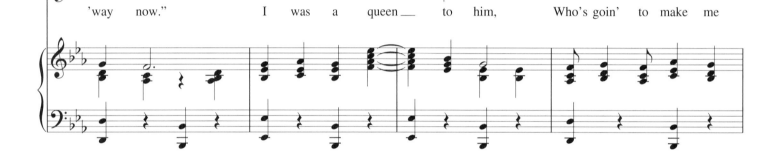

When I was mean ___ to him He'd nev - er say, "Go 'way now." I was a queen ___ to him, Who's goin' to make me

gay now? It's on - ly nat - 'ral I'm blue

ooo, He was too good ___ to be true. ___

For the complete song see: HL00308211 *The Best of Rodgers and Hart,* and other sources.

HOME

Excerpt

from Walt Disney's *Beauty and the Beast: The Broadway Musical*

Music by ALAN MENKEN
Lyrics by TIM RICE

For the complete song see: HL00312511 *Disney's Beauty and the Beast: The Broadway Musical* vocal selections, and other sources.

Excerpt
HOW LOVELY TO BE A WOMAN
from *Bye Bye Birdie*

Lyric by LEE ADAMS
Music by CHARLES STROUSE

For the complete song see: HL00313233 *Bye Bye Birdie* vocal selections.

Excerpt

HOW ARE THINGS IN GLOCCA MORRA
from *Finian's Rainbow*

Words by E.Y. HARBURG
Music by BURTON LANE

For the complete song see: HL00312138 *Finian's Rainbow* vocal selections, and other sources.

Excerpt

I BELONG HERE
from *The Grand Tour*

Music and Lyric by
JERRY HERMAN

For the complete song see: HL00385217 *The Jerry Herman Songbook.*

I COULD HAVE DANCED ALL NIGHT
from *My Fair Lady*

Words by ALAN JAY LERNER
Music by FREDERICK LOEWE

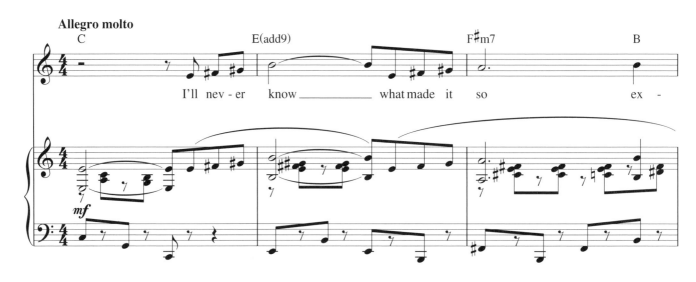

I'll nev-er know _____ what made it so ex-

cit - ing; _____ Why all at once my

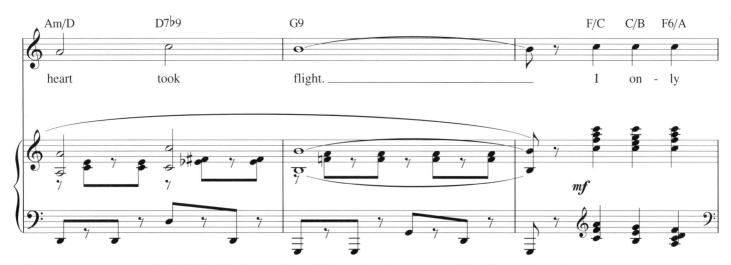

heart took flight. _____ I on-ly

For the complete song see: HL00361071 *The Singer's Musical Theatre Anthology, Soprano Vol. 1 (Revised)*, and other sources.

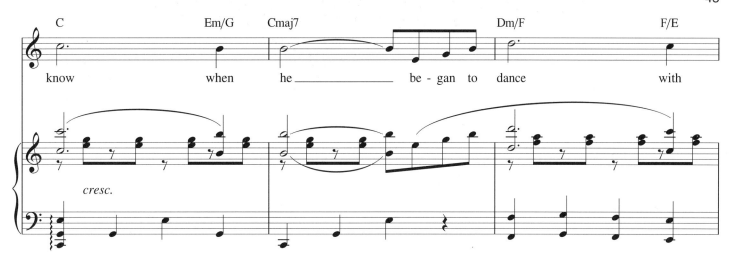

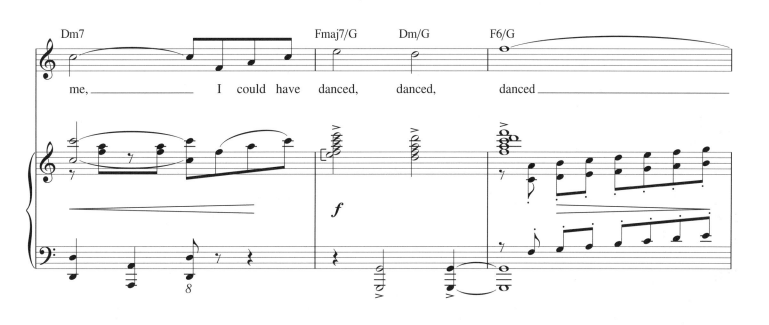

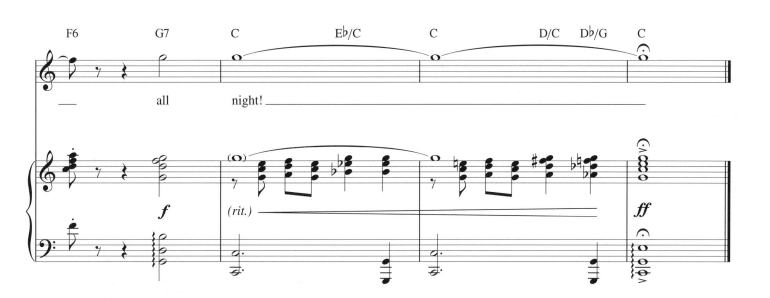

Excerpt

I COULD WRITE A BOOK
from *Pal Joey*

Words by LORENZ HART
Music by RICHARD RODGERS

For the complete song see: HL0074016 *The Songs of Richard Rodgers – High Voice,* and other sources.

Excerpt

I GOT LOST IN HIS ARMS

from *Annie Get Your Gun*

Words and Music by
IRVING BERLIN

For the complete song see: HL00005576 *Annie Get Your Gun* vocal selections, and other sources.

Excerpt

I HAVE DREAMED
from *The King and I*

Lyrics by OSCAR HAMMERSTEIN II
Music by RICHARD RODGERS

For the complete song see: HL00740081 *The First Book of Broadway Solos, Soprano,* and other sources.

Excerpt

I HAVE TO TELL YOU
from *Fanny*

Words and Music by
HAROLD ROME

For the complete song see: HL00312134 *Fanny* vocal selections.

I LIKE HIM
from *Drat! The Cat!*

Lyric by IRA LEVIN
Music by MILTON SCHAFER

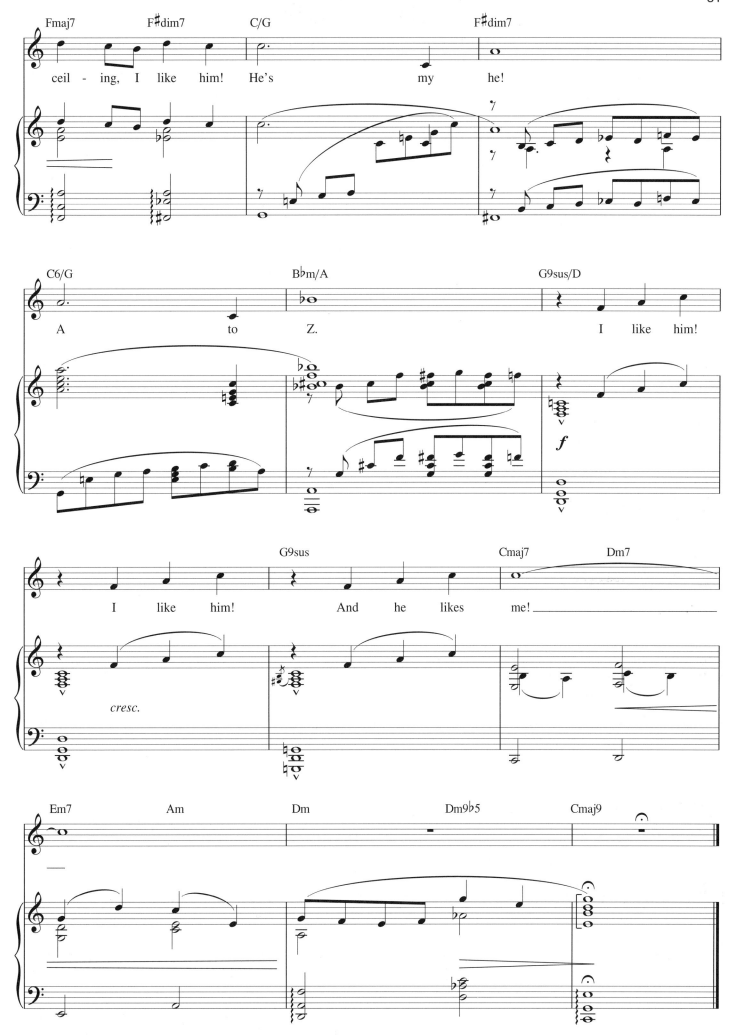

I WISH I DIDN'T LOVE YOU SO
from the Paramount Picture *The Perils of Pauline*

Words and Music by
FRANK LOESSER

For the complete song see: HL00444442 *The Frank Loesser Songbook,* and other sources.

Excerpt

I'LL KNOW
from *Guys and Dolls*

By FRANK LOESSER

For the complete song see: HL00747066 *The Singer's Musical Theatre Anthology, Soprano Vol. 2 (Revised),* and other sources.

Excerpt

I'LL SHOW HIM
from *Plain and Fancy*

Words by ARNOLD B. HORWITT
Music by ALBERT HAGUE

Excerpt

I'VE NEVER SAID I LOVE YOU

from *Dear World*

Music and Lyric by
JERRY HERMAN

For the complete song see: HL00383360 *Dear World* vocal selections, and other sources.

IF I LOVED YOU
from *Carousel*

Lyrics by OSCAR HAMMERSTEIN II
Music by RICHARD RODGERS

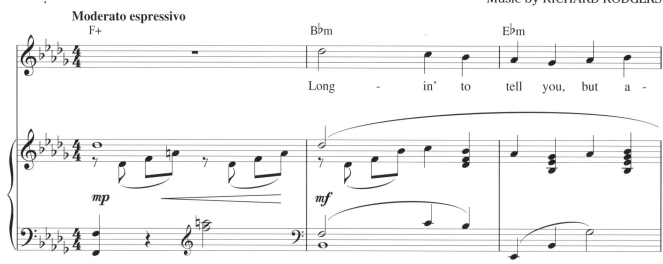

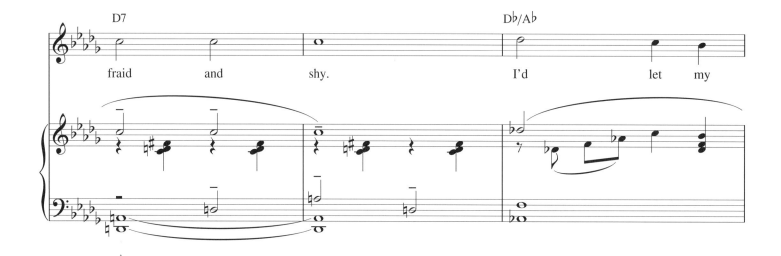

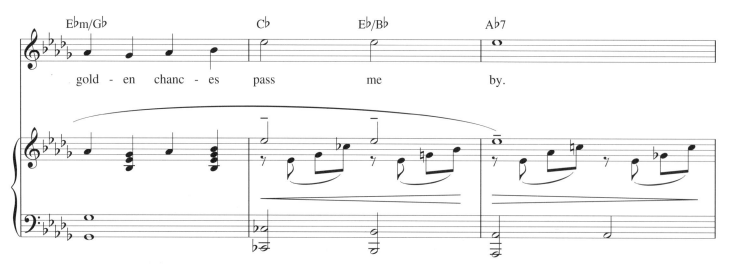

For the complete song see: HL00361071 *The Singer's Musical Theatre Anthology, Soprano Vol. 1 (Revised),* and other sources.

IN BUDDY'S EYES
(Buddy's There)
from *Follies*

Words and Music by
STEPHEN SONDHEIM

For the complete song see: HL00359869 *Follies* vocal selections, and other fources.

Excerpt

IN MY LIFE
from *Les Misérables*

Music by CLAUDE-MICHEL SCHÖNBERG
Lyrics by HERBERT KRETZMER
Original Text by ALAIN BOUBLIL and JEAN-MARC NATEL

For the complete song see: HL00740122 *The Singer's Musical Theatre Anthology, Soprano Vol. 3*, and other sources.

Excerpt

IN MY OWN LITTLE CORNER
from *Cinderella*

Lyrics by OSCAR HAMMERSTEIN II
Music by RICHARD RODGERS

For the complete song see: HL00740122 *The Singer's Musical Theatre Anthology, Soprano Vol. 3,* and other sources.

Excerpt
IT MIGHT AS WELL BE SPRING
from *State Fair*

Lyrics by OSCAR HAMMERSTEIN II
Music by RICHARD RODGERS

For the complete song see: HL00312403 *State Fair* vocal selections, and other sources.

Excerpt

IS HE THE ONLY MAN IN THE WORLD?

from *Mr. President*

Words and Music by
IRVING BERLIN

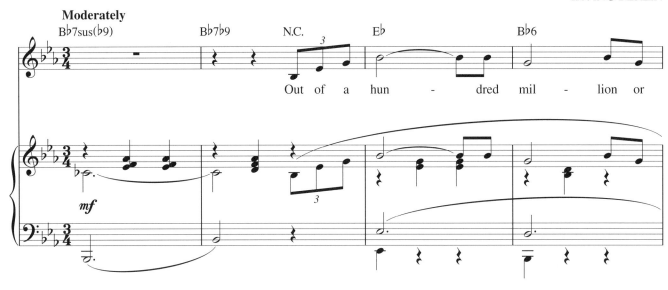

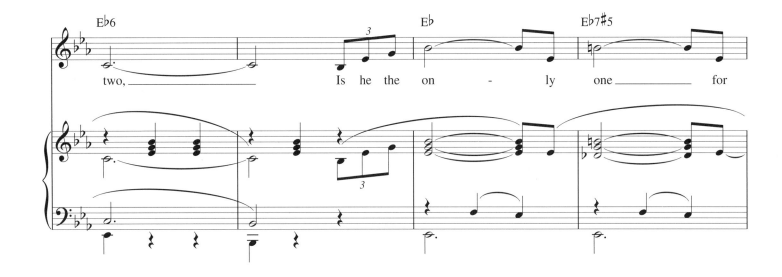

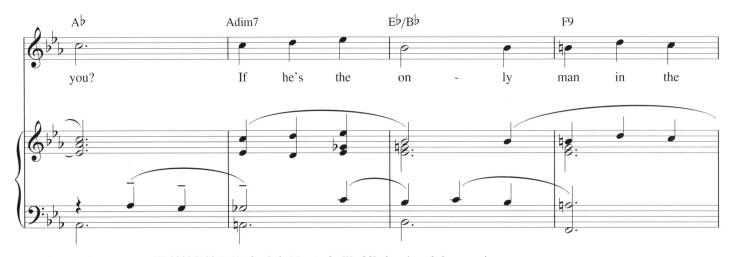

For the complete song see: HL00005122 *Is He the Only Man in the World?* piano/vocal sheet music.

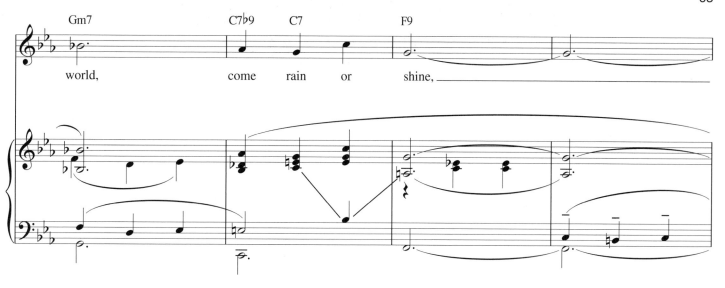

world, come rain or shine, _____

Then he's a man _____

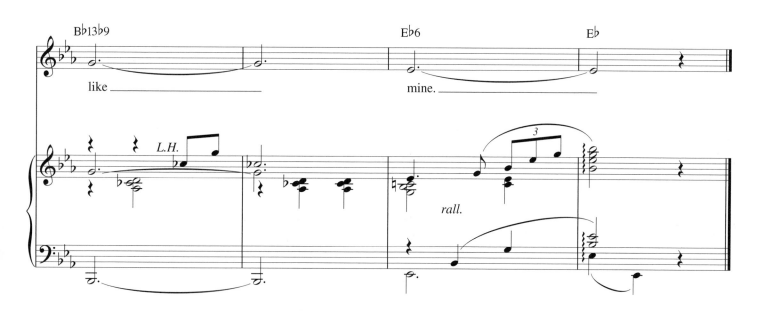

like _____ mine. _____

IT NEVER ENTERED MY MIND

from *Higher and Higher*

Words by LORENZ HART
Music by RICHARD RODGERS

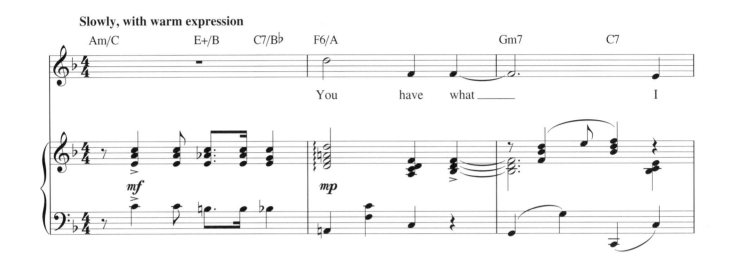

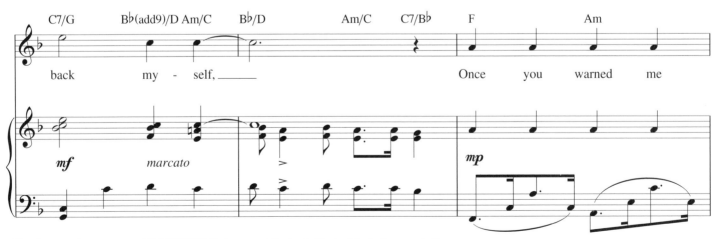

For the complete song see: HL00307940 *Rodgers and Hart – A Musical Anthology,* and other sources.

That if you scorned me, I'd sing the maid - en's pray'r a - gain

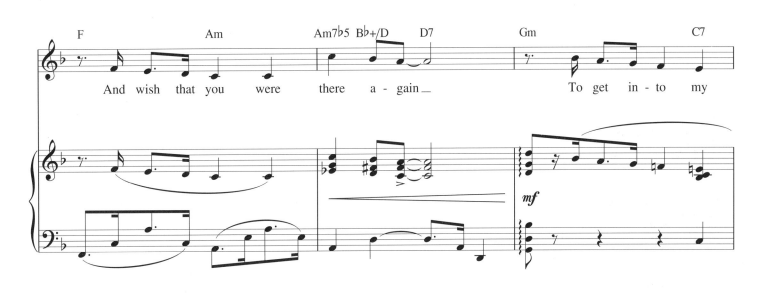

And wish that you were there a - gain To get in - to my

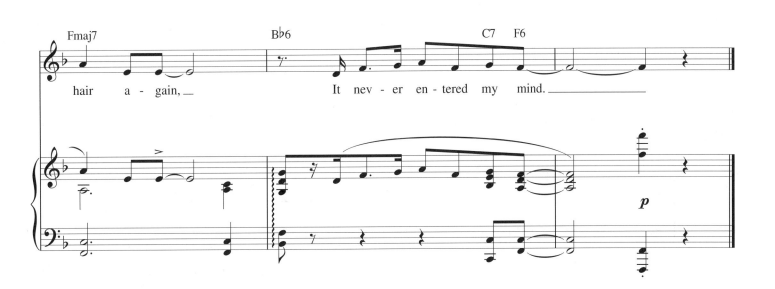

hair a - gain, It nev - er en - tered my mind.

IT'S A LOVELY DAY TODAY
from the Stage Production *Call Me Madam*

Words and Music by
IRVING BERLIN

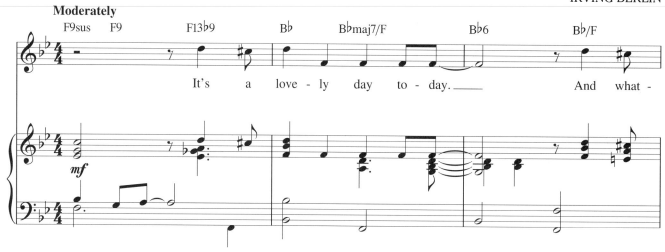

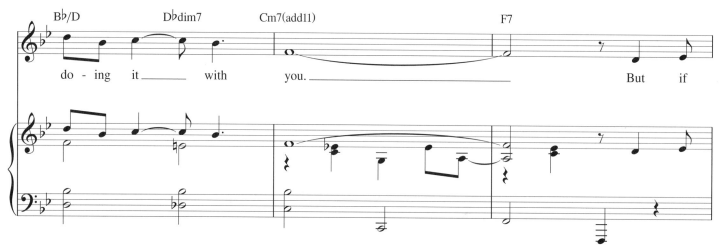

For the complete song see: HL00005577 *Call Me Madam* vocal selections, and other sources.

ITALIAN STREET SONG
from *Naughty Marietta*

Lyrics by RIDA JOHNSON YOUNG
Music by VICTOR HERBERT

For the complete song see: HL00740122 *The Singer's Musical Theatre Anthology, Soprano Vol. 3,* and other sources.

Excerpt

JUST IMAGINE
from *Good News*

Words and Music by B.G. DeSYLVA,
LEW BROWN and RAY HENDERSON

For the complete song see: HL00740081 *The First Book of Broadway Solos, Soprano.*

Excerpt

KISS HER NOW
from *Dear World*

Words and Music by
JERRY HERMAN

For the complete song see: HL00383360 *Dear World* vocal selections, and other sources.

Excerpt

LONG BEFORE I KNEW YOU

from *Bells Are Ringing*

Words by BETTY COMDEN and ADOLPH GREEN
Music by JULE STYNE

Lyrics:
All that was long be-fore I held you ____
Long be-fore I kissed you ____
Long be-fore I touched you ____ And felt this glow. ____
But now you real-ly are here and now at last I know,
That long be-fore I knew you ____ I loved you so. ____

For the complete song see: HL00361198 *The Songs of Jule Styne*, and other sources.

Excerpt

LOOK AT ME, I'M SANDRA DEE
(Reprise)
from *Grease*

Lyric and Music by WARREN CASEY
and JIM JACOBS

For the complete song see: HL00313103 *Grease Is Still the Word.*

Excerpt

LOVE, LOOK AWAY
from *Flower Drum Song*

Lyrics by OSCAR HAMMERSTEIN II
Music by RICHARD RODGERS

For the complete song see: HL00361071 *The Singer's Musical Theatre Anthology, Soprano Vol. 1 (Revised),* and other sources.

LOOK NO FURTHER
from *No Strings*

Lyrics and Music by
RICHARD RODGERS

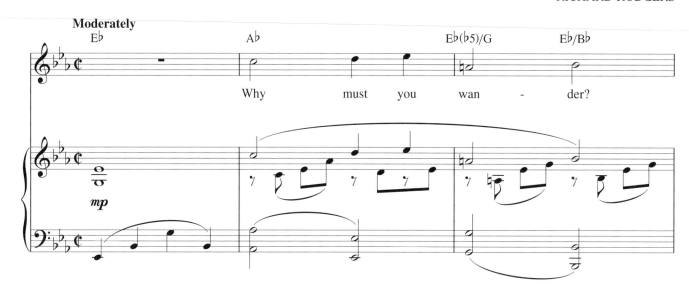

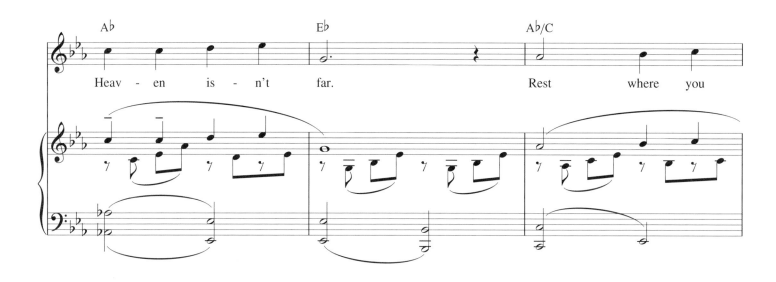

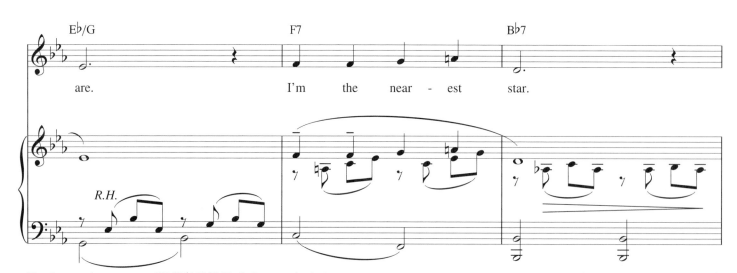

For the complete song see: HL00312280 *No Strings* vocal selctions.

Excerpt

LOOK TO THE RAINBOW
from *Finian's Rainbow*

Words by E.Y. HARBURG
Music by BURTON LANE

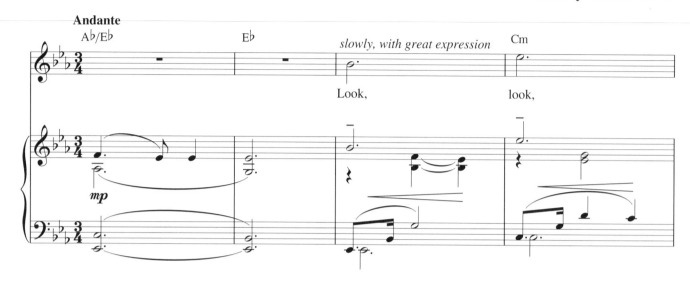

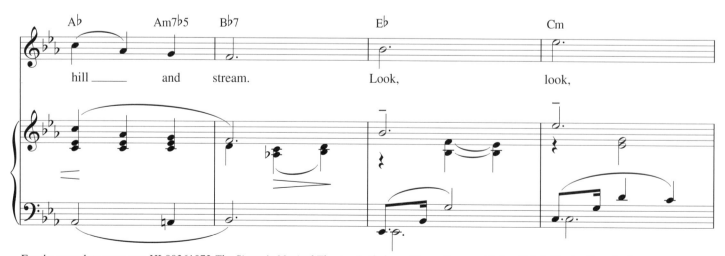

For the complete song see: HL00361072 *The Singer's Musical Theatre Anthology, Mezzo-Soprano/Belter Vol. 1 (Revised)*, and other sources.

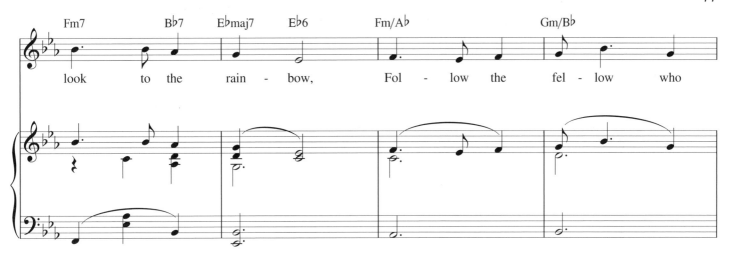

look to the rain - bow, Fol - low the fel - low who

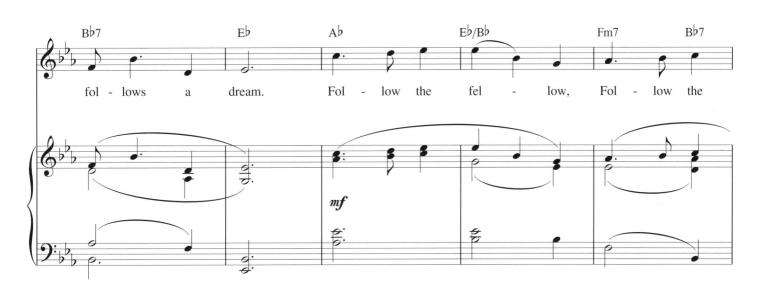

fol - lows a dream. Fol - low the fel - low, Fol - low the

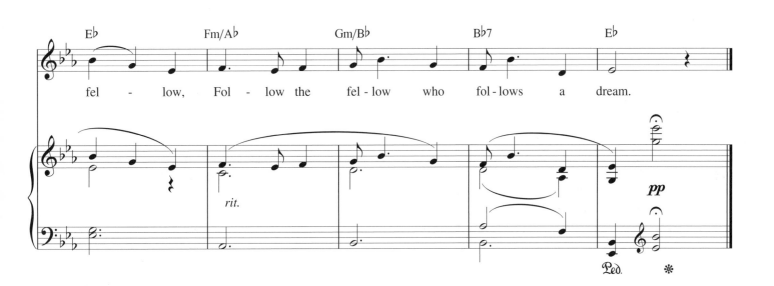

fel - low, Fol - low the fel - low who fol - lows a dream.

LOVE, DON'T TURN AWAY
from *110 in the Shade*

Words by TOM JONES
Music by HARVEY SCHMIDT

For the complete song see: HL00312303 *110 in the Shade* vocal selections.

Excerpt

LOVE SONG
from *Celebration*

Words by TOM JONES
Music by HARVEY SCHMIDT

For the complete song see: HL00312070 *Celebration* vocal selections, and other sources.

LOVELY
from *A Funny Thing Happened on the Way to the Forum*

Excerpt

Words and Music by
STEPHEN SONDHEIM

For the complete song see: HL00312151 *A Funny Thing Happened on the Way to the Forum* vocal selections.

LOVER, COME BACK TO ME

from *The New Moon*

Lyrics by OSCAR HAMMERSTEIN II
Music by SIGMUND ROMBERG

For the complete song see: HL00310561 *The Big Book of Torch Songs*, and other sources.

Excerpt

MAKE SOMEONE HAPPY
from *Do Re Mi*

Words by BETTY COMDEN
and ADOLPH GREEN
Music by JULE STYNE

For the complete song see: HL00361198 *The Songs of Jule Styne,* and other sources.

Excerpt

MISTER SNOW
from *Carousel*

Lyrics by OSCAR HAMMERSTEIN II
Music by RICHARD RODGERS

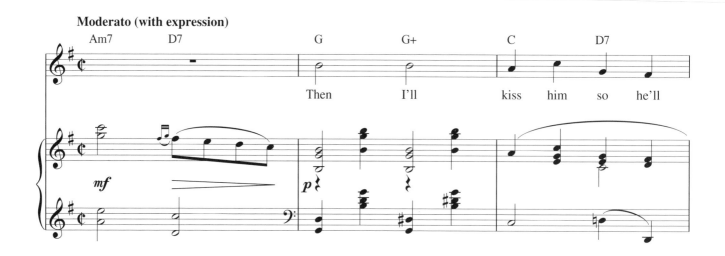

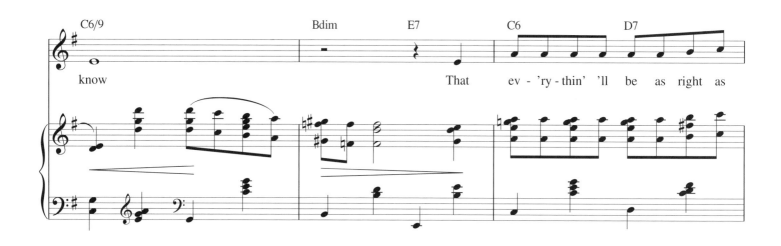

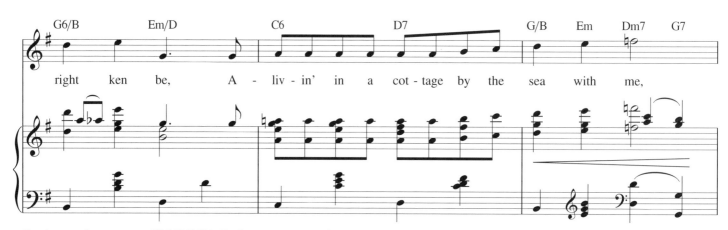

For the complete song see: HL00361071 *The Singer's Musical Theatre Anthology, Soprano Vol. 1 (Revised)*, and other sources.

MUCH MORE
from *The Fantasticks*

Words by TOM JONES
Music by HARVEY SCHMIDT

For the complete song see: HL00361071 *The Singer's Musical Theatre Anthology, Soprano Vol. 1 (Revised)*, and other sources.

Excerpt

MY LORD AND MASTER
from *The King and I*

Lyrics by OSCAR HAMMERSTEIN II
Music by RICHARD RODGERS

For the complete song see: HL00361071 *The Singer's Musical Theatre Anthology, Soprano Vol. 1 (Revised),* and other sources.

MY DARLING, MY DARLING
from *Where's Charley?*

By FRANK LOESSER

For the complete song see: HL00447285 *Where's Charley?* vocal selections, and other sources.

Excerpt

MY FUNNY VALENTINE
from *Babes in Arms*

Words by LORENZ HART
Music by RICHARD RODGERS

Slowly (with expression)

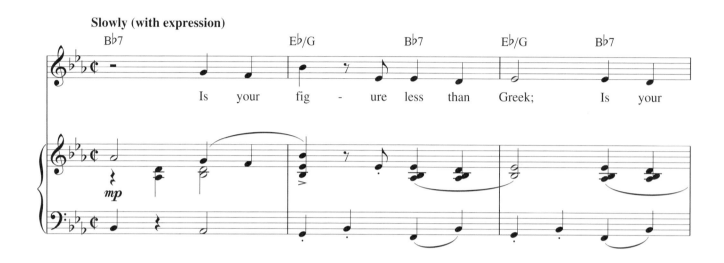

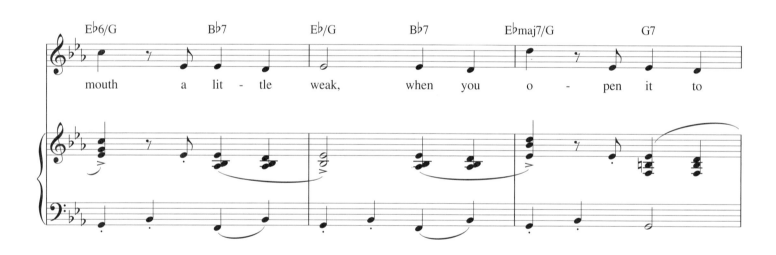

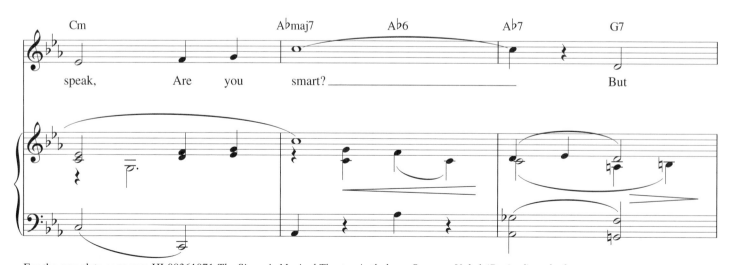

For the complete song see: HL00361071 *The Singer's Musical Theatre Anthology, Soprano Vol. 1 (Revised),* and other sources.

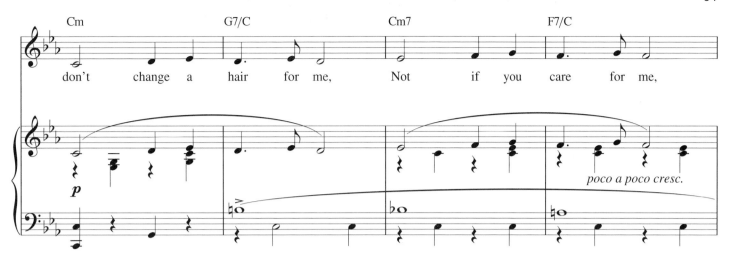

don't change a hair for me, Not if you care for me,

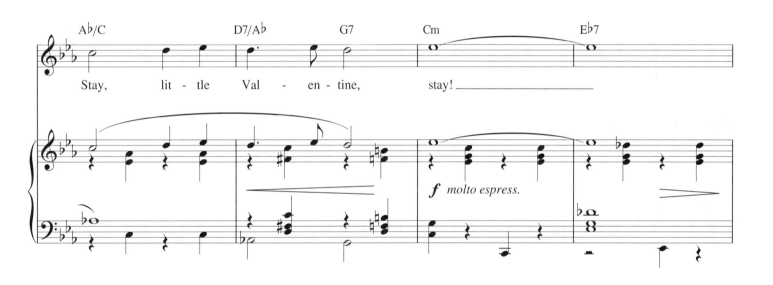

Stay, lit - tle Val - en - tine, stay! _____

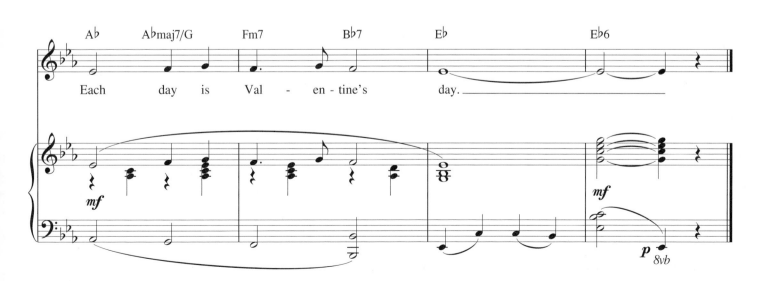

Each day is Val - en - tine's day. _____

MY ROMANCE

from *Jumbo*

Words by LORENZ HART
Music by RICHARD RODGERS

For the complete song see: HL00740166 *Songs of Richard Rodgers* - High Voice, and other sources.

Excerpt

MY SHIP
from the Musical Production *Lady in the Dark*

Words by IRA GERSHWIN
Music by KURT WEILL

For the complete song see: HL00361071 *The Singer's Musical Theatre Anthology, Soprano Vol. 1 (Revised)*, and other sources.

MY WHITE KNIGHT
from Meredith Willson's *The Music Man*

Words and Music by
MEREDITH WILLSON

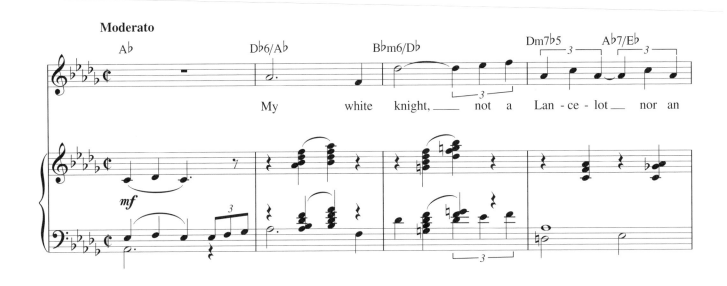

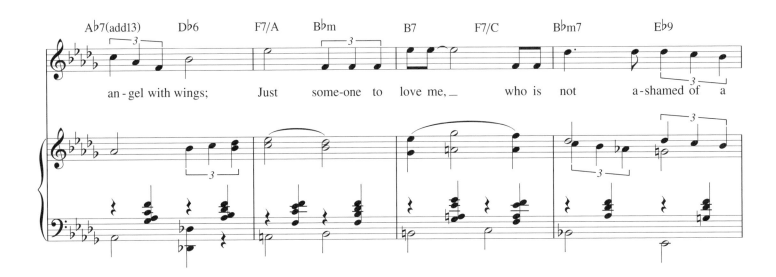

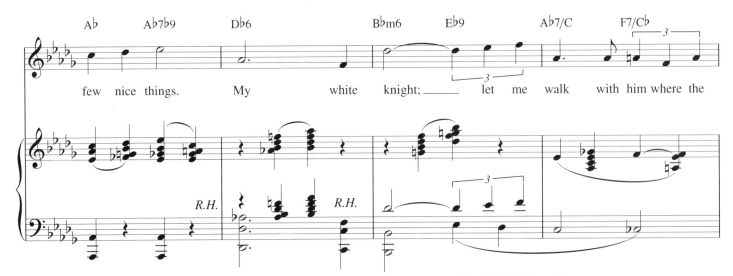

For the complete song see: HL00361071 *The Singer's Musical Theatre Anthology, Soprano Vol. 1 (Revised),* and other sources.

NEVER NEVER LAND
from *Peter Pan*

Lyric by BETTY COMDEN and ADOLPH GREEN
Music by JULE STYNE

Moderately (with expression)

You'll have a treas-ure if you stay there,

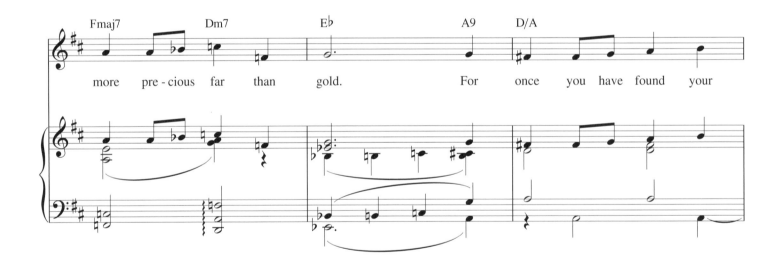

more pre-cious far than gold. For once you have found your

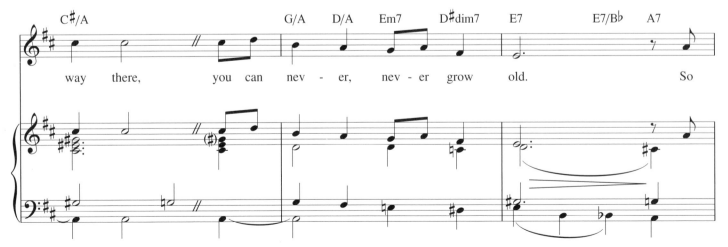

way there, you can nev - er, nev - er grow old. So

For the complete song see: HL00384551 *Peter Pan* vocal selections, and other sources.

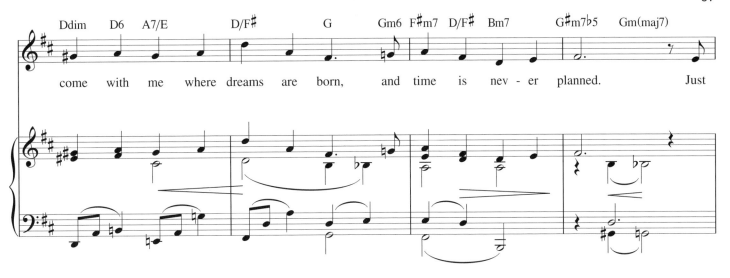

come with me where dreams are born, and time is nev-er planned. Just

think of love-ly things, and your heart will fly on wings, for-ev-er_____ in

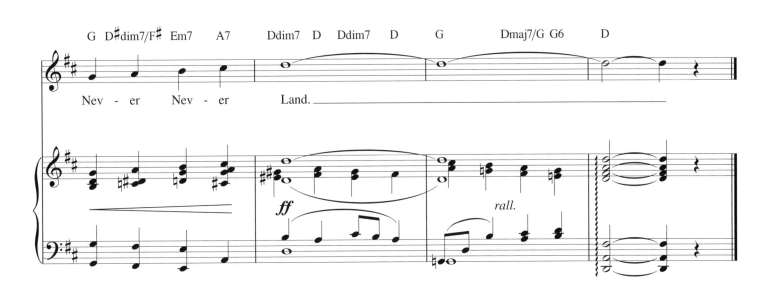

Nev-er Nev-er Land._____

MY TRUE LOVE

from *Phantom*

Words and Music by
MAURY YESTON

For the complete song see: HL00747066 *The Singer's Musical Theatre Anthology, Soprano Vol. 2 (Revised),* and other sources.

Excerpt

NOBODY TOLD ME
from *No Strings*

Lyrics and Music by
RICHARD RODGERS

For the complete song see: HL00312280 *No Strings* vocal selections.

Excerpt

ONCE YOU LOSE YOUR HEART

from *Me and My Girl*

Words and Music by
NOEL GAY

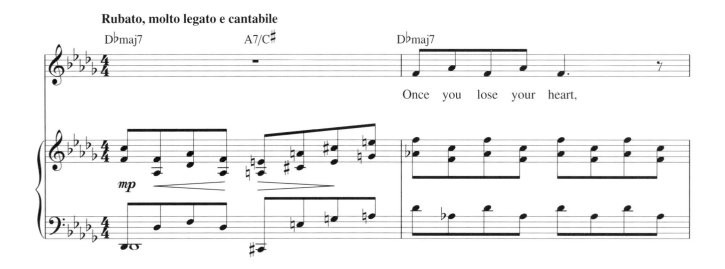

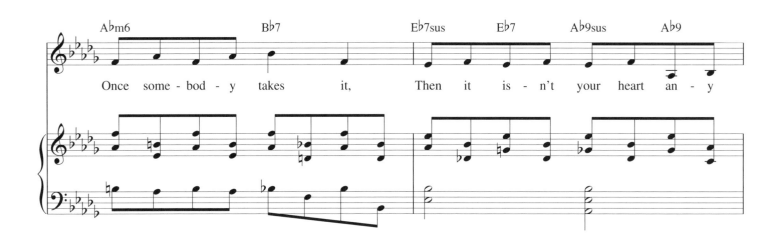

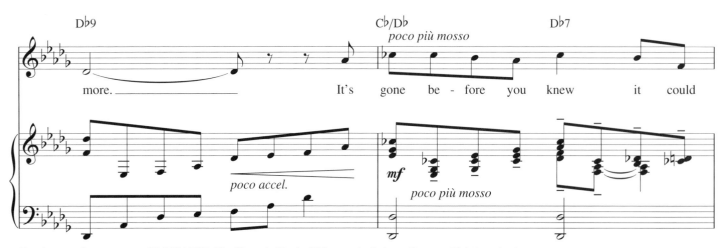

For the complete song see: HL00740122 *The Singer's Musical Theatre Anthology, Soprano Vol. 3,* and other sources.

Excerpt

ONE MORE KISS
from *Follies*

Words and Music by
STEPHEN SONDHEIM

Adagio, poco rubato (♩=120)

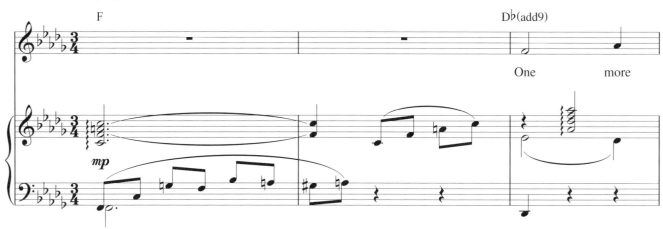

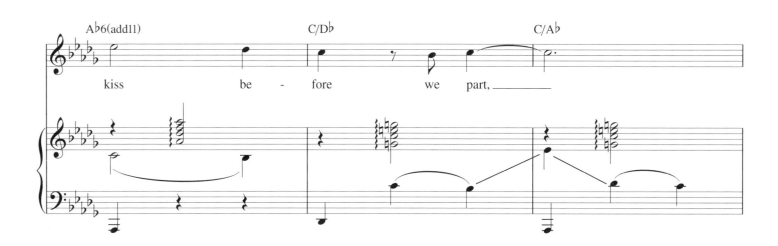

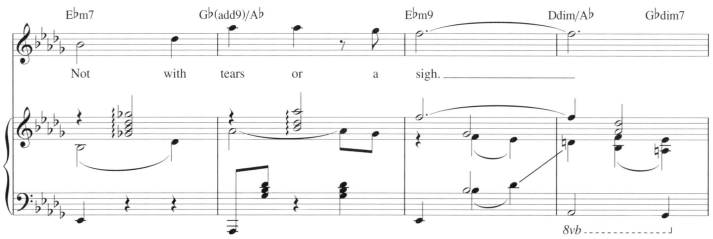

For the complete song see: HL00361071 *The Singer's Musical Theatre Anthology, Soprano Vol. 1 (Revised)*, and other sources.

All things _____ beau - ti - ful must die. _____

Now _____ that our love is done, _____

Lov - er give me one more kiss and good -

bye.

Excerpt

OUT OF MY DREAMS
from *Oklahoma!*

Lyrics by OSCAR HAMMERSTEIN II
Music by RICHARD RODGERS

Tempo di valse

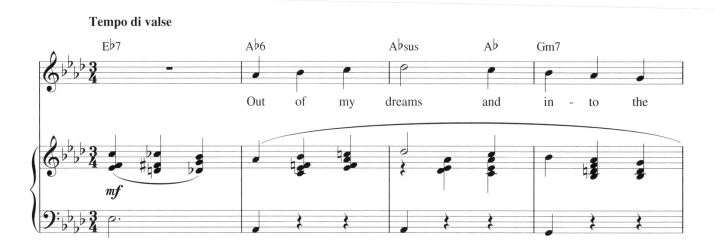

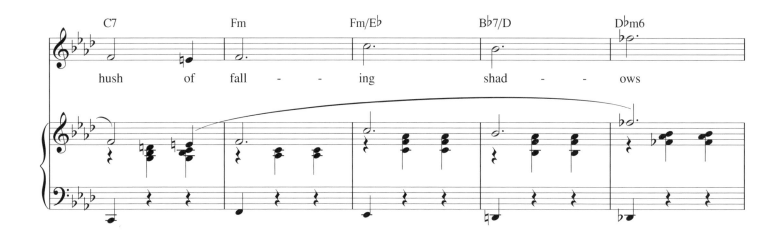

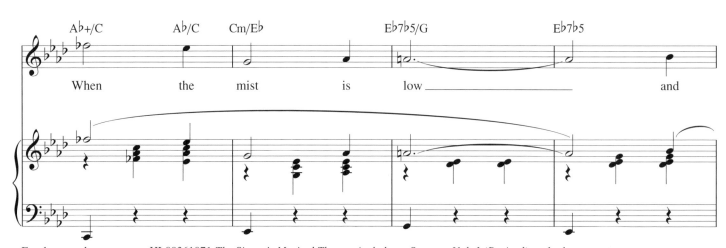

For the complete song see: HL00361071 *The Singer's Musical Theatre Anthology, Soprano Vol. 1 (Revised)*, and other sources.

Excerpt

PART OF YOUR WORLD
from Walt Disney's *The Little Mermaid*

Lyrics by HOWARD ASHMAN
Music by ALAN MENKEN

Moderately (with a beat)

For the complete song see: HL00313169 *Contemporary Disney,* and other sources.

Excerpt

ONE BOY
from *Bye Bye Birdie*

Lyric by LEE ADAMS
Music by CHARLES STROUSE

For the complete song see: HL00313233 *Bye Bye Birdie* vocal selections.

PEOPLE WILL SAY WE'RE IN LOVE

Excerpt

from *Oklahoma!*

Lyrics by OSCAR HAMMERSTEIN II
Music by RICHARD RODGERS

For the complete song see: HL00312292 *Oklahoma!* vocal selections, and other sources.

RIBBONS DOWN MY BACK

from *Hello, Dolly!*

Music and Lyric by
JERRY HERMAN

Slowly (in 2)

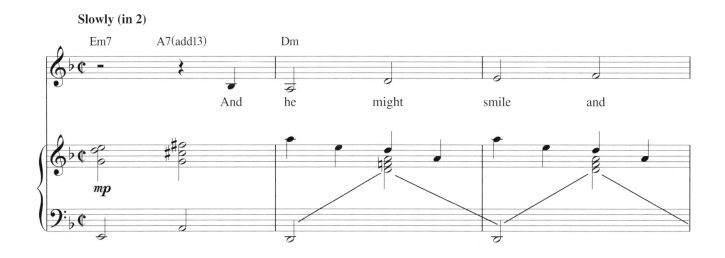

And he might smile and

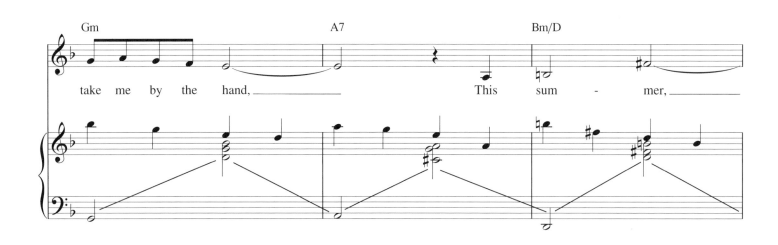

take me by the hand, _____ This sum - mer, _____

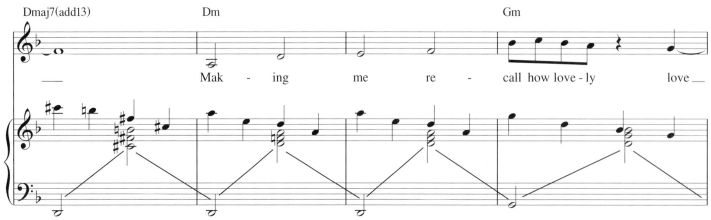

_____ Mak - ing me re - call how love - ly love ___

For the complete song see: HL00740122 *The Singer's Musical Theatre Anthology, Soprano Vol. 3*, and other sources.

Excerpt

SHOW ME
from *My Fair Lady*

Words by ALAN JAY LERNER
Music by FREDERICK LOEWE

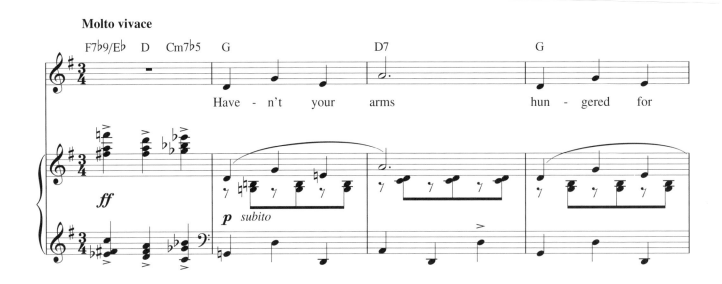

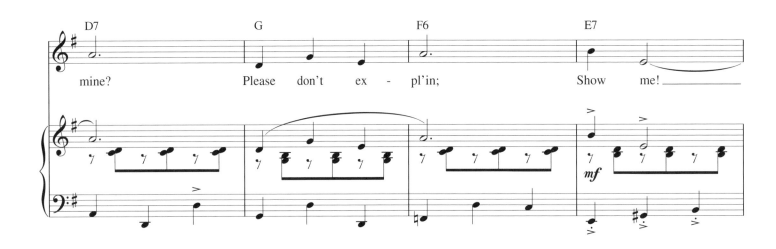

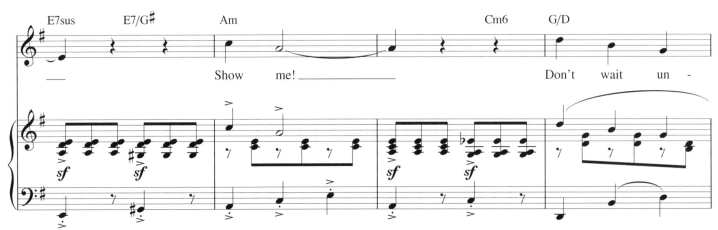

For the complete song see: HL00361071 *The Singer's Musical Theatre Anthology, Soprano Vol. 1 (Revised)*, and other sources.

THE SIMPLE JOYS OF MAIDENHOOD

Excerpt

from *Camelot*

Words by ALAN JAY LERNER
Music by FREDERICK LOEWE

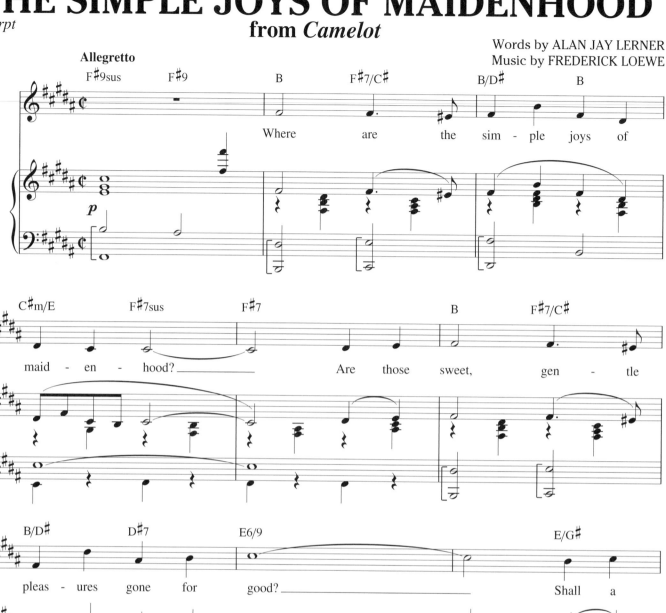

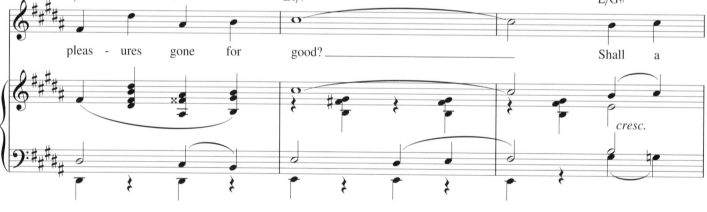

For the complete song see: HL00361071 *The Singer's Musical Theatre Anthology, Soprano Vol. 1 (Revised)*, and other sources.

SIMPLE LITTLE THINGS
from *110 in the Shade*

Words by TOM JONES
Music by HARVEY SCHMIDT

For the complete song see: HL00747066 *The Singer's Musical Theatre Anthology, Soprano Vol. 2 (Revised)*, and other sources.

Excerpt

SO FAR
from *Allegro*

Lyrics by OSCAR HAMMERSTEIN II
Music by RICHARD RODGERS

Moderato

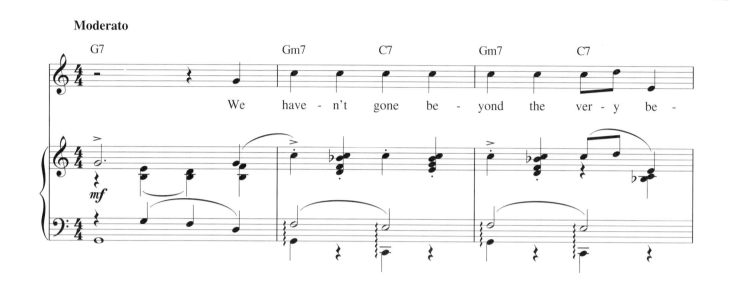

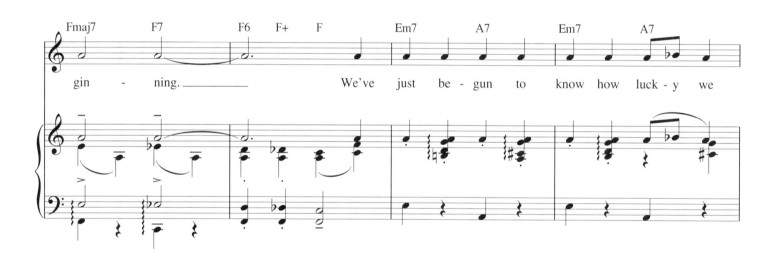

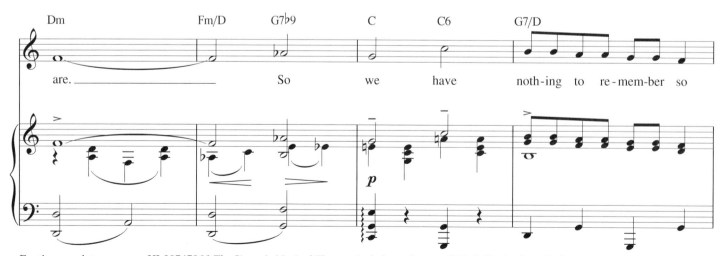

For the complete song see: HL00747066 *The Singer's Musical Theatre Anthology, Soprano Vol. 2 (Revised),* and other sources.

119

SO IN LOVE
from *Kiss Me, Kate*

Words and Music by
COLE PORTER

For the complete song see: HL00361071 *The Singer's Musical Theatre Anthology, Soprano Vol. 1 (Revised),* and other sources.

Excerpt

SO MANY PEOPLE
from *Saturday Night*

Music and Lyrics by
STEPHEN SONDHEIM

For the complete song see: HL00740122 *The Singer's Musical Theatre Anthology, Soprano Vol. 3,* and other sources.

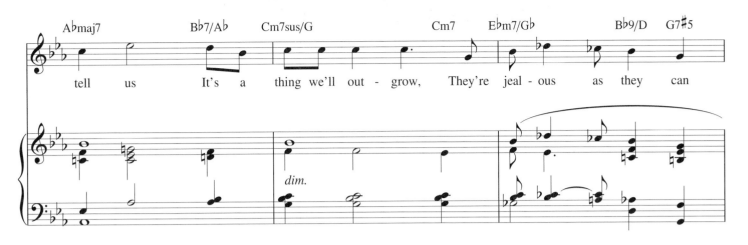

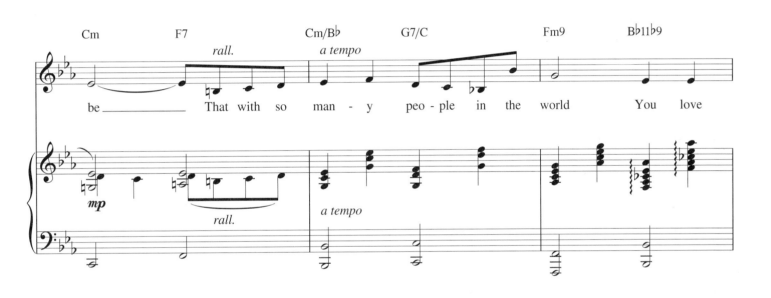

SOMEBODY, SOMEWHERE
from *The Most Happy Fella*

By FRANK LOESSER

For the complete song see: HL00361071 *The Singer's Musical Theatre Anthology, Soprano Vol. 1 (Revised),* and other sources.

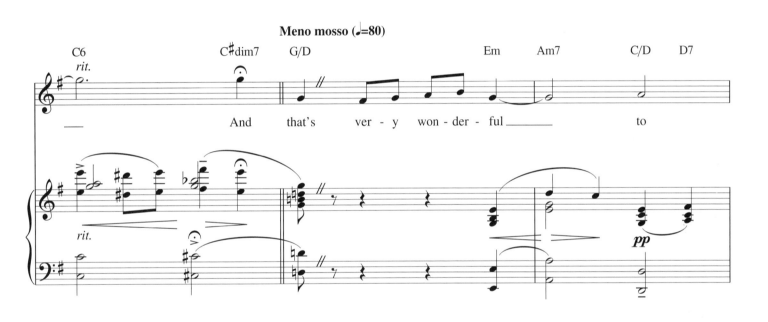

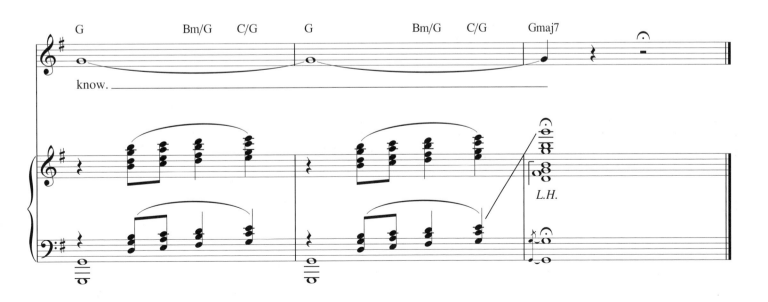

Excerpt

SOMEONE NICE LIKE YOU
from the Musical Production *Stop the World - I Want to Get Off*

Words and Music by LESLIE BRICUSSE
and ANTHONY NEWLEY

For the complete song see: HL00310386 *Love Songs from Broadway.*

Excerpt

SOMETHING THERE
from Walt Disney's *Beauty and the Beast: The Broadway Musical*

Lyrics by HOWARD ASHMAN
Music by ALAN MENKEN

For the complete song see: HL00312511 *Disney's Beauty and the Beast: The Broadway Musical vocal selections*, and other sources.

SOMETHING WONDERFUL
from *The King and I*

Lyrics by OSCAR HAMMERSTEIN II
Music by RICHARD RODGERS

For the complete song see: HL00361071 *The Singer's Musical Theatre Anthology, Soprano Vol. 1 (Revised)*, and other sources.

He'll al - ways need your love, And so he'll

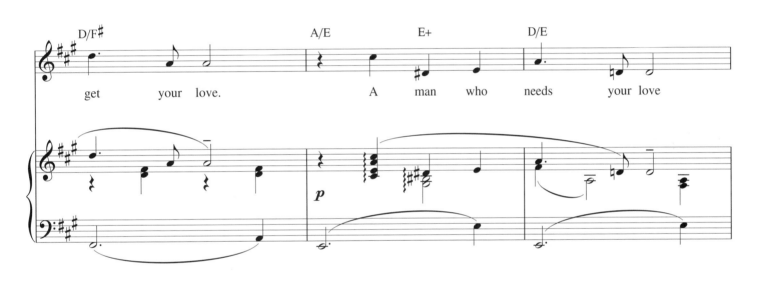

get your love. A man who needs your love

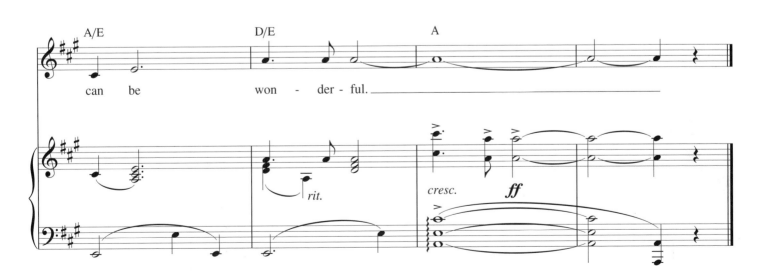

can be won - der - ful.

THE SOUND OF MUSIC

from *The Sound of Music*

Lyrics by OSCAR HAMMERSTEIN II
Music by RICHARD RODGERS

For the complete song see: HL00747066 *The Singer's Musical Theatre Anthology, Soprano Vol. 2 (Revised)*, and other sources.

Excerpt

SPEAK LOW
from the Musical Production *One Touch of Venus*

Words by OGDEN NASH
Music by KURT WEILL

For the complete song see: HL00361124 *Songs of the '40s,* and other sources.

TEN MINUTES AGO
from *Cinderella*

Lyrics by OSCAR HAMMERSTEIN II
Music by RICHARD RODGERS

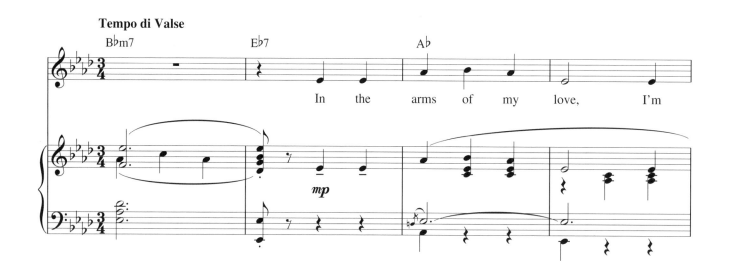

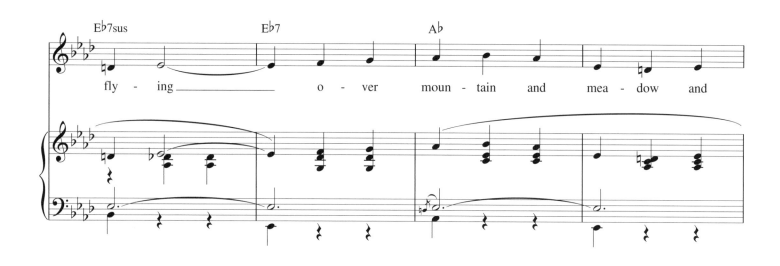

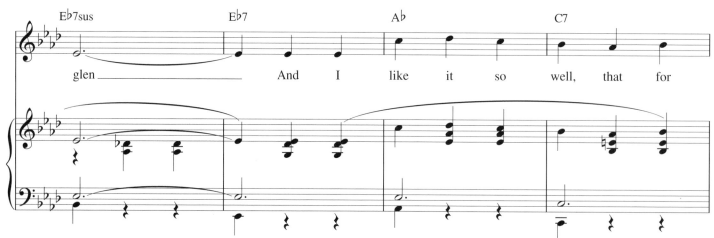

For the complete song see: HL00361071 *The Singer's Musical Theatre Anthology, Soprano Vol. 1 (Revised)*, and other sources.

THAT'LL SHOW HIM
from *A Funny Thing Happened on the Way to the Forum*

Words and Music by
STEPHEN SONDHEIM

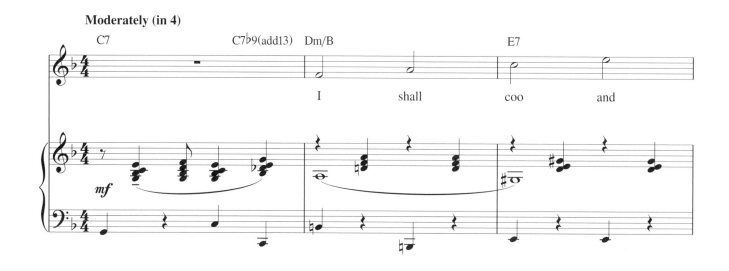

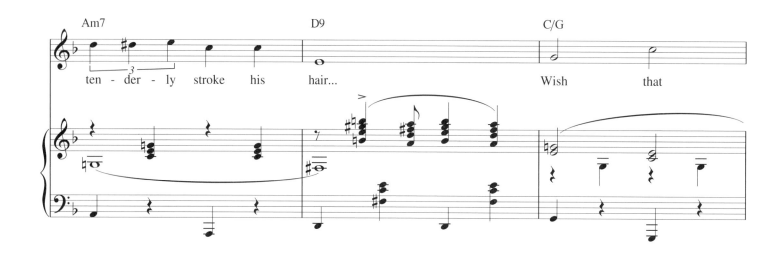

For the complete song see: HL00361071 *The Singer's Musical Theatre Anthology, Soprano Vol. 1 (Revised)*, and other sources.

Excerpt

TILL THERE WAS YOU
from Meredith Willson's *The Music Man*

By MEREDITH WILLSON

Moderato e rubato

And there was mu-sic and

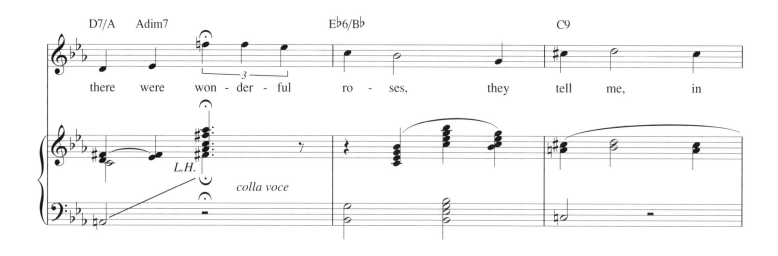

there were won-der-ful ro-ses, they tell me, in

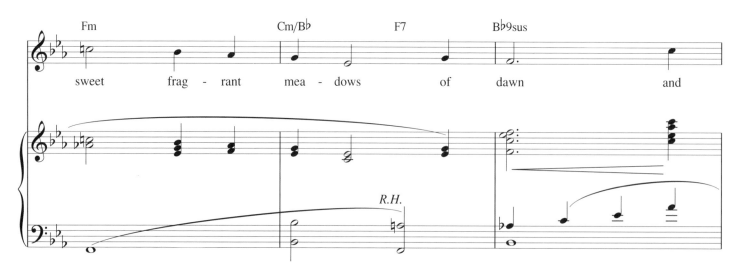

sweet frag-rant mea-dows of dawn and

For the complete song see: HL00361071 *The Singer's Musical Theatre Anthology, Soprano Vol. 1 (Revised),* and other sources.

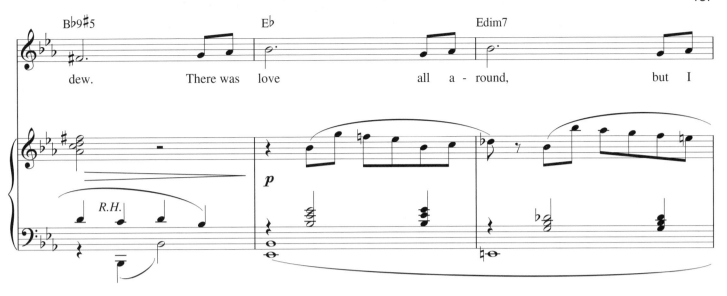

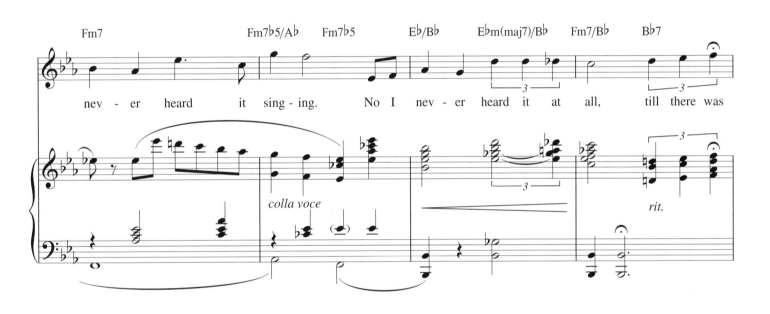

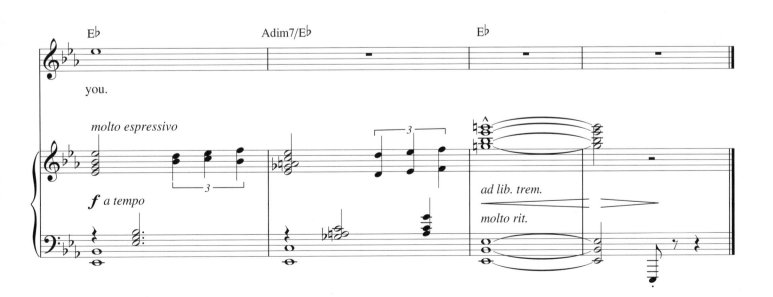

TOO MUCH IN LOVE TO CARE

from *Sunset Boulevard*

Music by ANDREW LLOYD WEBBER
Lyrics by DON BLACK and CHRISTOPHER HAMPTON

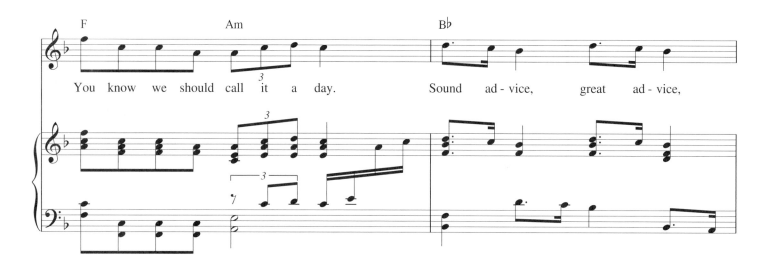

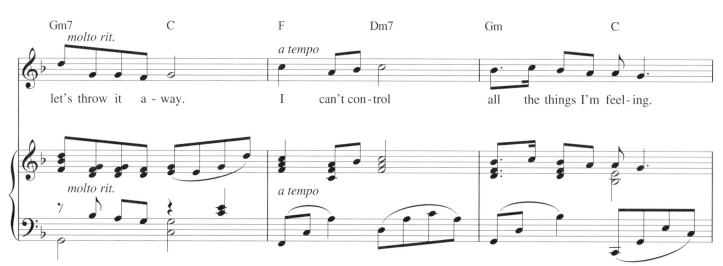

For the complete song see: HL00312514 *Sunset Boulevard* vocal selections, and other sources.

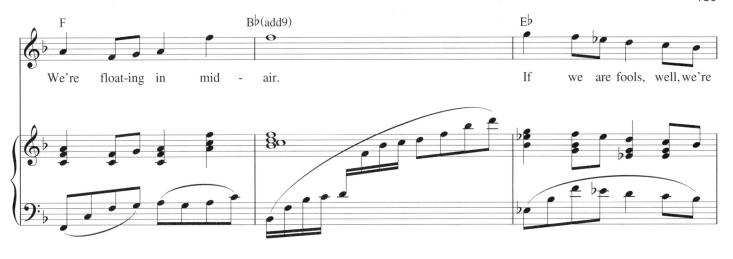

We're float-ing in mid - air. If we are fools, well, we're

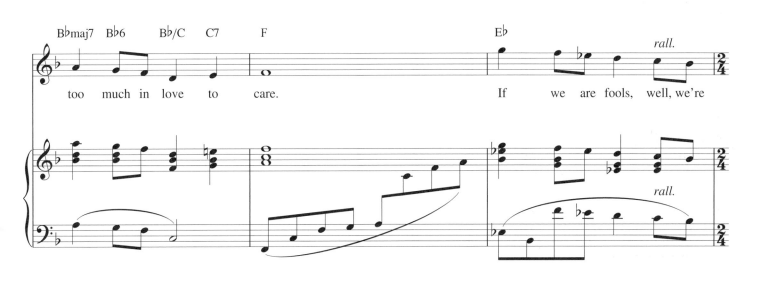

too much in love to care. If we are fools, well, we're

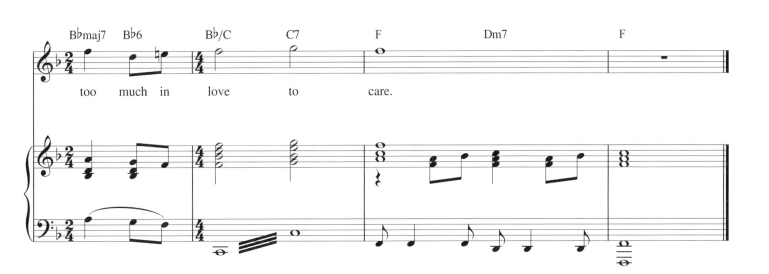

too much in love to care.

Excerpt

UNUSUAL WAY
(In A Very Unusual Way)
from *Nine*

Words and Music by
MAURY YESTON

For the complete song see: HL00747066 *The Singer's Musical Theatre Anthology, Soprano Vol. 2 (Revised)*, and other sources.

THERE'S NO REASON IN THE WORLD

Excerpt

from *Milk and Honey*

Music and Lyric by
JERRY HERMAN

For the complete song see: HL00384251 *Milk and Honey vocal selections*, and other sources.

Excerpt

WARM ALL OVER
from *The Most Happy Fella*

By FRANK LOESSER

For the complete song see: HL00747066 *The Singer's Musical Theatre Anthology, Soprano Vol. 2 (Revised),* and other sources.

WHAT GOOD WOULD THE MOON BE?

Excerpt

from the Musical Production *Street Scene*

Words by LANGSTON HUGHES
Music by KURT WEILL

Moderato (with warm expression)

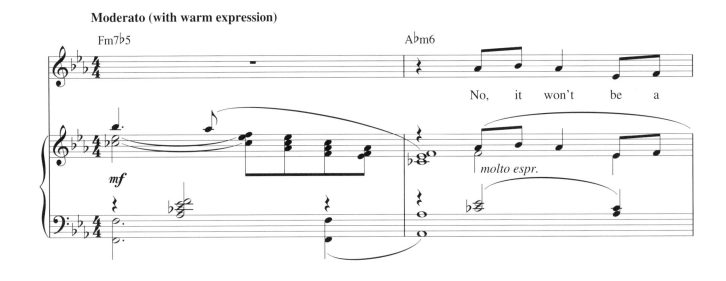

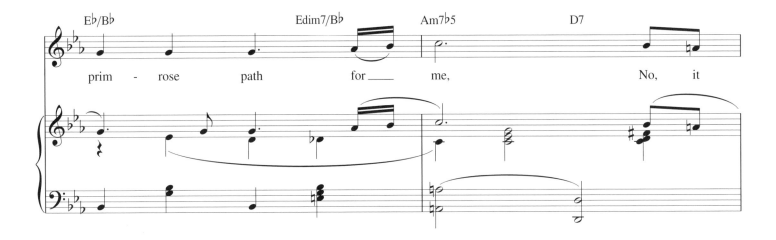

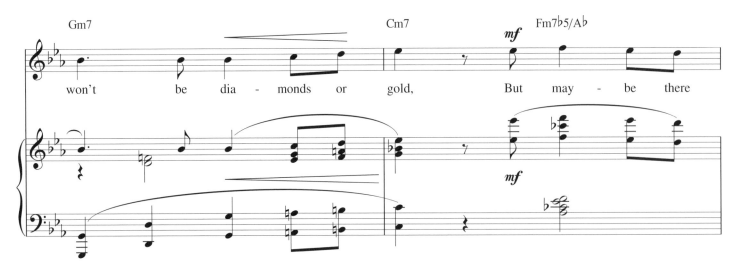

For the complete song see: HL00361071 *The Singer's Musical Theatre Anthology, Soprano Vol. 1 (Revised),* and other sources.

145

WHAT IS A WOMAN?
from *I Do! I Do!*

Words by TOM JONES
Music by HARVEY SCHMIDT

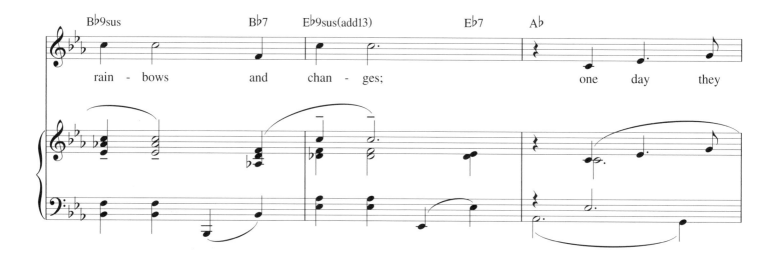

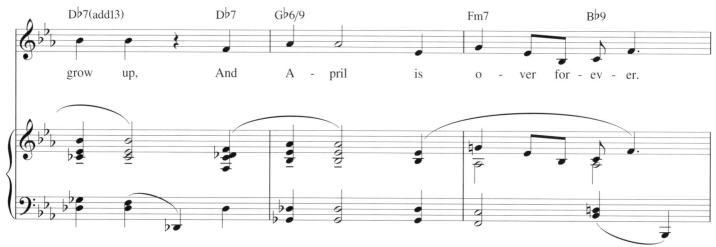

For the complete song see: HL00312207 *I Do! I Do!* vocal selections, and other sources.

WHEN SHE LOVED ME
from Walt Disney Pictures' *Toy Story 2 - A Pixar Film*

Music and Lyrics by
RANDY NEWMAN

For the complete song see: HL00313169 *Contemporary Disney,* and other sources.

WHERE, OH WHERE

from *Out of This World*

Words and Music by
COLE PORTER

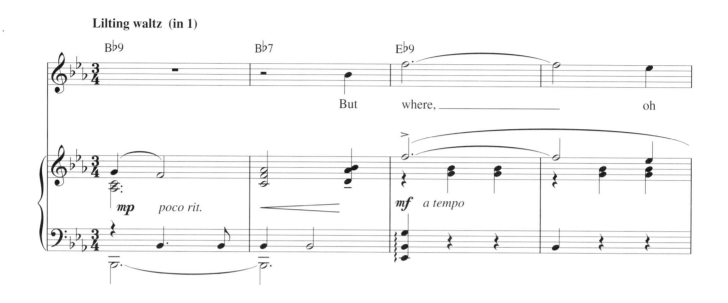

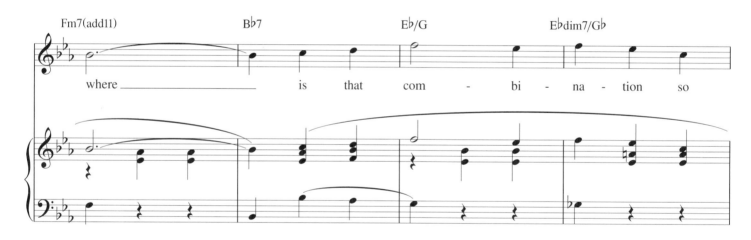

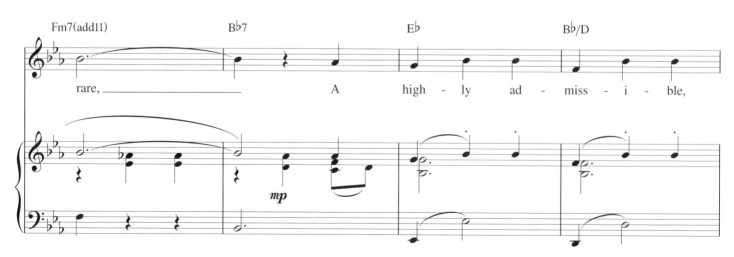

For the complete song see: HL00311630 *Broadway Comedy Songs,* and other sources.

WHERE OR WHEN
from *Babes in Arms*

Words by LORENZ HART
Music by RICHARD RODGERS

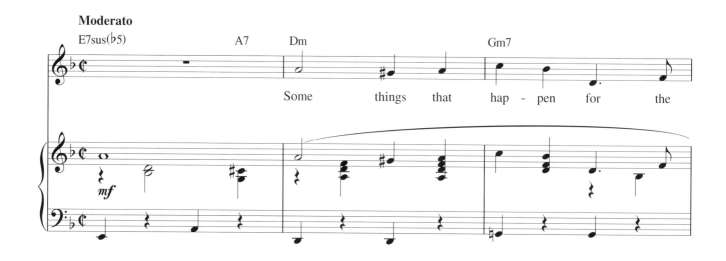

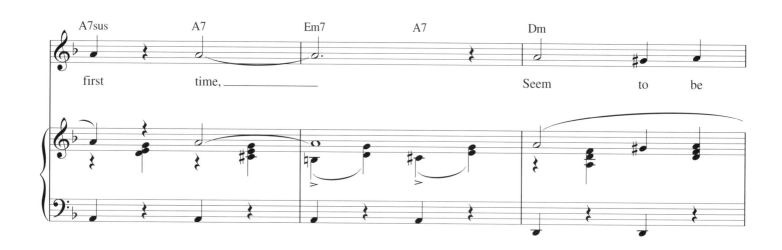

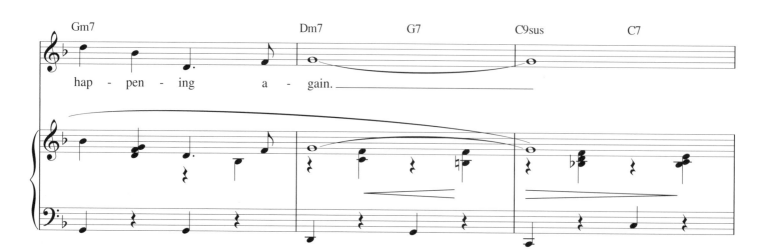

For the complete song see: HL00361071 *The Singer's Musical Theatre Anthology, Soprano Vol. 1 (Revised),* and other sources.

Excerpt

WHO ARE YOU NOW?
from *Funny Girl*

Words by BOB MERRILL
Music by JULE STYNE

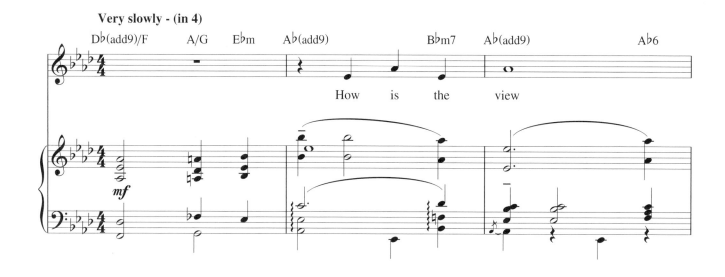

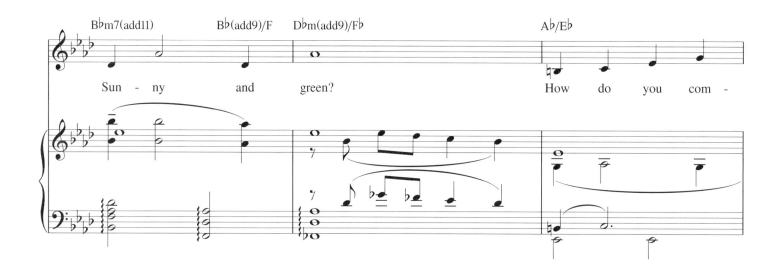

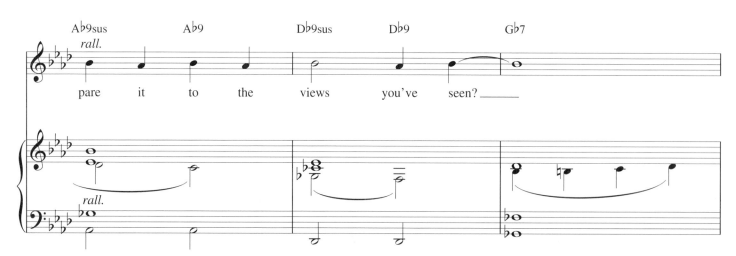

For the complete song see: HL00312149 *Funny Girl* vocal selections, and other sources.

YOU DON'T KNOW THIS MAN
from *Parade*

Music and Lyrics by
JASON ROBERT BROWN

Poco Rubato throughout (♩ = 116)

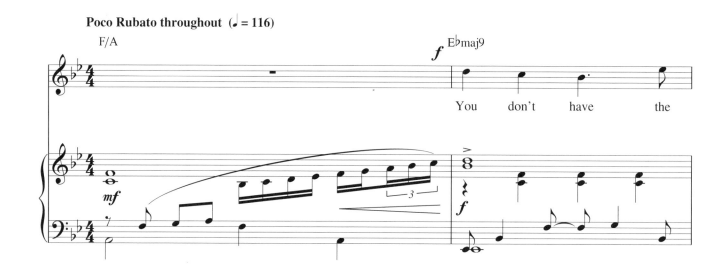

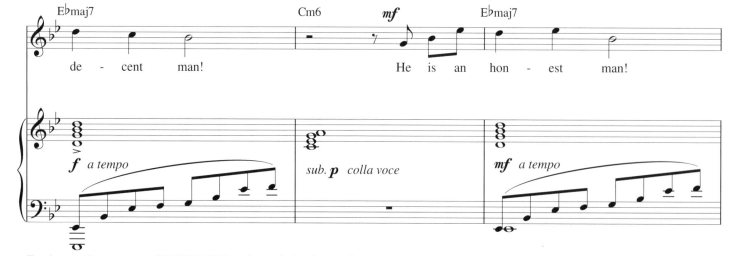

For the complete song see: HL00313148 *Parade* vocal selections, and other sources.

YOU'LL NEVER WALK ALONE
from *Carousel*

Lyrics by OSCAR HAMMERSTEIN II
Music by RICHARD RODGERS

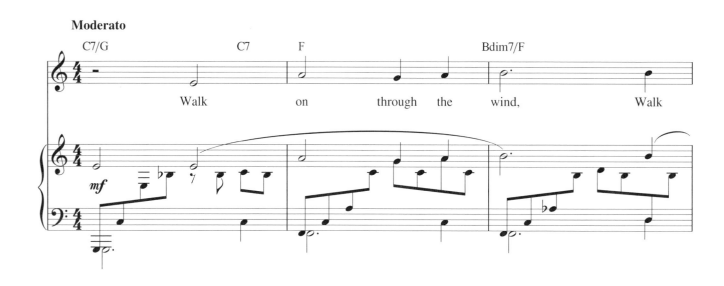

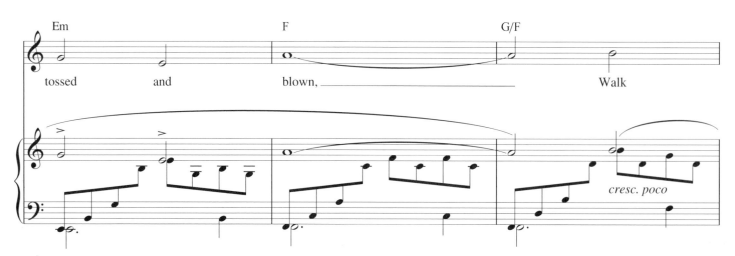

For the complete song see: HL00361071 *The Singer's Musical Theatre Anthology, Soprano Vol. 1 (Revised),* and other sources.